From Gutted *to* Glorious

PRAISE FOR *FROM GUTTED TO GLORIOUS*

"*From Gutted to Glorious* is a radiant gem in the world of grief, mental health, and wellness. With wit, wisdom, and raw honesty, Jennifer Hacker transforms heartbreak into a masterclass on healing. This isn't just a book about surviving loss—it's about embracing it as a gateway to living more fully. Her journey from devastation to restoration is both deeply personal and profoundly universal. It's not just a read; it's a companion for anyone ready to rise from the ashes and rediscover joy—with heart, humor, and hope."
—Jodi Wellman, MAPP, Author of *You Only Die Once*

"As a genetic counselor, I have helped many families navigate grief associated with genetic diagnosis and familial illness. With her book, Jennifer Hacker gives us a gift that moves us beyond the academic literature about grief; she opens her heart and shares her wisdom as a life and grief coach in a way that's empowering and transformative. Her personal narrative will draw you in, make you laugh out loud, and shed more than a few tears. You'll feel like she's your bestie who's unafraid to tell it like it is—and she gives you actionable, practical advice to help you move beyond grief. If you're grieving or supporting someone who is, this book is an elixir for your heart."
—Mary Pritzlaff, MS, CGC

"As a mental health and energy release therapist, I've witnessed countless expressions of grief, and one universal truth emerges: No one experiences the same path to healing. Jennifer masterfully guides readers through the authentic grief process, abandoning outdated stage models for a more intuitive approach that honors individual experiences. Her revolutionary Grief Transformation Model isn't about 'getting over' loss but rather honoring the spaces we inhabit throughout our grief journey. Jennifer's compassionate voice emanates from every page, ensuring readers never feel alone as they navigate toward a balanced life. This isn't just another book on grief—it's a breakthrough in how we understand and process life's inevitable transitions."

–Rebecca Thorne, LCSW, BCC, The Art of Expansion

"To be alive is to experience grief–and to face one's grief is to come back more fully alive. In this clear-eyed, empathic, immensely helpful book, Jennifer Hacker names and counters society's myths and mistakes when it comes to grieving. Through her story and numerous helpful examples, she shows how navigating loss is doable and essential to living a meaningful, robust life. In the author's words: 'Your well-being and happiness are worth fighting for.' This book gives those experiencing loss a roadmap for doing just that."

–Jane Carter, M.Ed., Licensed Clinical Mental Health Counselor

"After reading far too many books on grief and healing that left me no closer to any form of peace, *From Gutted to Glorious* freed me to see the loss of my son and the loss of my decades-long marriage in a different light. Instead of pretending I'm okay, I can allow grief to change me into a better version of myself, the best version. Working through the six G's is a pathway to living and thriving. This book showed me that my broken pieces give meaning to my life, and they can guide me to a greater purpose than I could have ever imagined for my life, a glorious life!"

–Samantha Kriegel, ICF Certified Life Coach

"As a fellow griever, I really appreciate *From Gutted to Glorious*. I found it raw and honest, with many helpful suggestions on how to process the agonizing pain of child loss or any other painful event. Jennifer's personal story showed me that joy and purpose are possible after any deep emotionally painful loss. Her knowledge and wisdom came through on every page, leading me to have hope, strength, and courage to seek joy once again and to reach for my purpose.

As a fellow grief specialist, I feel more equipped to share the tools and knowledge shared in this book and will highly recommend it to my clients."

    –Sandra Frost, Certified (Advanced) Grief Recovery Specialist

"This book provides a new approach to living with and growing from the forever-walk of grief. If you've read virtually all the other approaches and found little solace or comfort, there are truths in these pages that will resonate with your healing soul. You will learn to live with and find comfort in this process! *From Gutted to Glorious* is a guidebook for rising from the ashes— learning to love the new and unanticipated you and thriving, not just surviving, through it all."

    –Samantha Anna, Mom to Zachary (forever 4 months old)

From Gutted *to* Glorious

**Transform Your Grief
and Rediscover Your Joy**

Jennifer J. Hacker

Publishing support provided by
Ignite Press
55 Shaw Ave. Suite 204
Clovis, CA 93612
www.IgnitePress.us

ISBN: 979-8-9989963-0-6
ISBN: 979-8-9989963-1-3 (Hardcover)
ISBN: 979-8-9989963-2-0 (E-book)

For bulk purchases and for booking, contact:

Jennifer Hacker
info@jenniferhacker.com
jenniferhacker.com

Library of Congress Control Number: 2025909368

Cover design by Ibrahem Ghareib
Edited by Zoe Herold
Interior design by Eswari Kamireddy

FIRST EDITION

To the 3 J's I honor with the 'J' in Jennifer J. Hacker:

"I'll be there beside you, for always, in all ways." –Kenny Loggins,
Always, In All Ways

Jackson – You made me a mom. You changed everything about who I was and who I am. You taught me that grief isn't a life sentence or a punishment; it's the sacred honoring of love.

Jayme and Jake – You are my joy, multiplied a thousand times over. You shape everything about who I am and who I'm becoming. I'm endlessly proud of you both and profoundly grateful to be your mom.

And to Johnny – My partner, my biggest fan, my prince.

"While the darkness has purpose, it is not meant to be your forever place. There is a new way to do grief. A way rooted in hope, and possibility with the promise of a new, joy-filled life. Say yes. Say yes. Say yes. To life. To love. To you."

— Tom Zuba, *Permission to Mourn*

Contents

INTRODUCTION

I sat in my office on a sunny Tuesday afternoon furiously trying to catch up on the slew of work that accumulated while I was on maternity leave.

Piles of paper surrounded me, stacked like teetering Jenga towers about to topple over. My phone intercom buzzed, and the receptionist said, "Your babysitter on Line 2."

Then came that feeling… the one where your heart drops out of your chest. You know your life will be forever changed by the very next thing that happens. On June 3, 2003, my ignorant bliss ended.

My three-month old son, Jackson, went down for a nap and never woke up. The cause of death was Sudden Infant Death Syndrome (SIDS) which basically means, "We can find no reason or explanation for why your seemingly healthy child is dead."

Thus began a long journey through unbelievable pain, endless *why?*'s, sleepless nights, re-evaluating *everything* (because nothing could be counted on ever again), losing my old self, and figuring out who my new self was going to be. I set off on a terrifying path filled with sadness and fear.

Years later, when my father died, I was detached and distant, hiding behind the walls I'd subconsciously erected to protect myself from additional pain. But after years and years, and doing the work of deep healing, I came to a place I thought I'd never be again, to living a meaningful, happy, purpose-filled, glorious life.

I wrote *From Gutted to Glorious* to give hope to those suffering grief and loss. You *can* survive, heal, and be gloriously fulfilled in life again. If you're wondering how I can make such a bold assertion, it's because, not only do I speak from personal experience, as a certified grief specialist, I've helped many clients find deep healing in the same ways that I have.

What This Book is About

The Health and Wellness and Mental Health industries are teeming with buzzwords like "self-care" and "inner work." Yet leading experts in these fields don't consider the role of grief in wellness. They prescribe anti-depressants or anti-anxiety medications and recommend practices like CBT (Cognitive Behavioral Therapy) without understanding that much of people's suffering can be traced back to the wounds of unresolved grief. This massive oversight is a product of our society's aversion to learning or talking about grief.

In today's culture, people avoid grief conversations like a moist hand coated in sneezy droplets: "Nope. Not touching that with a 13-foot pole." The purpose of this book is to alter society's aversion and position grief as an everyday topic, as common as discussing your favorite book or weekend plans.

"The way we deal with grief in our culture is broken," writes Megan Devine in *It's OK That You're Not OK*. She continues, "Our culture sees grief as a kind of malady: a terrifying, messy emotion that needs to be cleaned up and put behind us as soon as possible. As a result, we have outdated beliefs around how long grief should last and what it should look like."

The scale of the problem Devine describes is staggering. The office of the Assistant Secretary for Planning and Evaluation (ASPE) reported to Congress in 2023 that the number of people experiencing grief has dramatically increased due to the pandemic: "… as of July 2023, there have been over 1.1 million deaths from COVID-19, and for every COVID-19 death there are an average of nine individuals who are bereaved."[1]

That's nine million new grievers since 2023 from the pandemic alone. When you add the increasing number of deaths by suicide and drug overdose, the numbers become even more overwhelming.

Another layer, on top of everything referenced above, is the fact that we've misunderstood grief for centuries and believed it to be exclusively about death. Death is only one catalyst of emotional pain. We experience grief in the wake of any significant loss, trauma, or transition.

I put grief into two categories. One is *death-related grief* which encompasses death-related losses (of people *and* pets). The other category is *life-transition grief*, which is a catch-all for other painful losses that result from major life transitions like divorce, the end of friendships, unemployment, new careers, empty nest, moving, menopause, etc.

So, which kind of grief do people deal with more often? *Life-transition grief*, right? Yet most people experience it without ever acknowledging or attending to the pain over these losses. Our society is extremely limited in that *death-related grief* is the only type we know about and talk about… *after it happens* (and only then if there's no identifiable escape from the dreaded conversation).

People avoid grief conversations like a moist hand coated in sneezy droplets: "Nope. Not touching that with a 13-foot pole."

With millions of new grievers entering our communities each year, and countless more struggling silently through life upheavals, we must do better to support all types of grievers in our culture. The need to understand grief and grievers isn't just increasing; it is urgent.

One significant way society can do better is understand that unresolved emotional pain is the underlying cause of many illnesses. As Bessel van der Kolk writes in *The Body Keeps the Score*, these illnesses include high blood pressure, anxiety, depression, heart attacks, chiropractic issues, ulcers, digestion issues, and many more. While these illnesses can be medically treated, getting to the root of the problem is the key to meaningful and long-lasting healing and health.

This is precisely why we need a new approach to grief. This book offers a path to that root-level healing. Rather than merely teaching that you will adjust and acclimate to living in the world again with time, interacting in supportive relationships, and other ill-defined theories, I write about the transformation that comes from progressing through my model – The 6 G's of Grief Transformation.

What to Expect in This Book

Throughout *From Gutted to Glorious* I share personal stories of loss and grief, as well as those of my clients (details altered to maintain confidentiality), which I hope will inspire you to think of the painful experiences and events in your life with a new perspective. You'll also find research-backed information, thought-provoking ideas, and a general guide to help you pave your own journey from Gutted to Glorious.

While you may read this book front-to-back, you may also hop around to chapters that feel most relevant to you today. The first chapter provides my grief origin story and my turning point to accidental grief transformation. Chapter 2 breaks down six common misbeliefs about grief that confound grievers in the healing process. Then you'll find an overview of my 6 G's of Grief Transformation in Chapter 3, followed by six chapters that break down the journey from Gutted to Glorious. Chapters 10 and 11 walk you through my grief transformation story at a granular level, and the final chapter considers guilt, letting go of both guilt and pain, without letting go of your loved one, and searching for peace.

If You're Supporting Someone in Grief

If you love someone who's grieving and want to help but don't know how, *this book will give you a window into their world.* You will gain invaluable insight into what grief really looks like… the messy, non-linear, *long* journey. You'll understand why your loved one doesn't "move on" according to expected timelines, learn what truly helps versus what inadvertently hurts, and discover how to show up as a healing presence.

Who This Book is For

I wrote this book for people who aren't sure if they can be fully healed after loss, yet they want to believe it's possible and are willing to take steps toward this goal. Notice I said "willing" instead of "ready." *You don't have to feel ready to heal and move forward, only that you're willing to try.*

You may be grieving the death of a close loved one or a big life-change such as divorce and what that change required you to leave behind. You may be a personal development junkie looking for the next step in your life's evolution. In any case, most likely some time has passed after your initial loss, and you were told you should be "over it" by now, yet grief still weighs heavy on your heart.

You know that losing someone means losing the 'you' that person brought out and the person you were with them in your life. There's no returning to *normal.* No "new normal" either. The word, "normal," often triggers emotional pain because *nothing* will ever be normal again. And the outside world just doesn't understand, especially if several years have passed, if you're mourning a pet, or you have no community where you can share your grief.

Life may feel 'as good as it gets' today, but that doesn't feel good enough. Jodi Wellman writes about this yearning for more in *You Only Die Once,* saying: "People in this category have life in them—so that's good—and yet there are also spots where they're missing a bit of vitality and meaning."

Perhaps you want to feel fulfilled on a new level. As Wellman writes, you might say, "I want more from life but I don't know how to get it." If so, you've probably found a level of homeostasis at home and work, and you're participating in life pretty well. But, you know something's still "off."

Maybe you're a veteran at hiding from the pain and pretending to feel better because it's been years since your loss occurred. Your emotional walls are up, and you're not asking friends or loved ones for support. What more support is there?

You read all the books, perhaps starting with *Good Grief*; the info was helpful but basic. Well-meaning people kept telling you about the "stages of grief" so you read *On Death and Dying* by Elisabeth Kübler-Ross. Those stages made some sense but didn't quite resonate with your experience. Maybe you felt more understood after reading David Kessler's book, *Finding Meaning* or Alan Wolfelt's *Healing a Grieving Heart,* but you walked away without much hope for the future. And you desperately want to find it.

You don't just feel broken. You feel like a core element was carved out of you. People call it a hole, but that word barely touches it. It's more like a sacred chamber… one you protect, because filling it feels like forgetting, or even betraying.

These misgivings hold you back from even thinking about additional healing, much less actually seeking it. But seek it, you must.

Grief transformation will not come knocking on your door like a new neighbor and offer you a plate of chocolate chip cookies. You may not feel ready but you want to take action, or at least to reconsider the "shoulds" of grief that make your continued pain feel wrong.

You may feel the shattered pieces of your heart are roughly held together but still aren't whole. Because this is just how life is after someone you love so much dies or you lose something huge that defined you.

Ultimately, you're probably in the grey area of healing. You've done some grief work, have healed to some extent, and overall, you're as happy as you think you can be. But deep down, there's still tremendous pain… a wound that seems untouchable.

Who This Book is Not For

Healing is an active pursuit, not passive. Time won't heal your wounds, ever. Not if all you're doing is waiting and wishing. If your heart is still so raw and tender that it's upsetting to hear stories about people finding happiness and meaning after loss, this book is likely not the tool for you (yet). This may not be the right time if your predominant thoughts are like these:

- *I admire the evolved people who can see the positive. I don't feel it. I am erupting with anger.*
- *I have no interest in doing anything, especially not running marathons or starting charities.*
- *I feel robbed and punished.*

If any of these sound like your current emotional state, you might need more time. And I'm not here to rush you. At some point you'll reach that critical moment, where you think, *"Okay, I want to move forward... somehow."* That's when you can retrieve this book and discover the benefits to be found.

Healing is an active pursuit, not passive. Time won't heal your wounds, ever.

From Gutted to Glorious can be there for you on standby, waiting until you get to the point that you want to feel better *and* you're willing to:

- Lean into learning, even when it's difficult and uncomfortable.
- Open your heart to the stories of others who've walked through trauma and loss.
- Welcome new ideas, new methods of healing, and the people who'll help you find them.

This book is not a substitute for mental health support. With grief, there are warning signs of serious mental health issues to be on the lookout for: alcohol or drug abuse and thoughts of suicide.

Now, wishing you could be with your loved one is not the same as being suicidal. Many grievers, myself included, have thought, "I wish

I wouldn't wake up tomorrow." But thinking about *harming* yourself is different.

If you're seriously considering suicide, set this book down right now and talk to a mental health professional. If you feel like hurting yourself, call the nationwide 988 Suicide & Crisis Lifeline: 1-800-273-TALK (8255). It provides 24/7 support for individuals in suicidal crisis or emotional distress.

If you're feeling unsure, afraid of change, or of facing your big emotions and "letting go," I understand. That's why I've included a whole section in this book to walk you through those fears. For now, please just keep reading and stay open to what's ahead.

You deserve this transformational journey of self-discovery, honoring your pain, reconciling your past so you can embrace the future, and moving forward into joy and purpose without 'moving on.'

If you take away nothing else from reading this introduction, know that I never thought feeling glorious was possible, either, but I did it. And *you* can too!

ONE

MY JOURNEY FROM GUTTED TO GLORIOUS

Joy and peace are miracles. Twenty years ago, I thought I'd never experience either feeling ever again. This chapter tells the story of my infant son's death and how I went from being completely gutted and trying to heal, to finding a place of hope for better days.

For many years, I misunderstood the grief process, which kept me stuck in hiding and heartache. Still, I forged ahead on my grief journey and emerged feeling better than I thought possible, and now I have the privilege of helping others heal their deepest grief wounds.

J.R.R. Tolkien offers a powerful metaphor, applicable to the grief journey, in *The Two Towers*. Frodo, the hobbit, is tasked with destroying the ring of power to save the free world and his home. He doubts that he can complete his mission. Then his closest friend, Sam, says:

> "It's like in the great stories, Mr. Frodo. The ones that really mattered, full of darkness and danger, they were. And sometimes you didn't want to know the end, because how could the end be happy?… But in the end, it's only a passing thing, this shadow. Even darkness must pass. A new day will come.

And when the sun shines, it will shine out the clearer. Those were the stories that stayed with you… Folk in those stories had lots of chances of turning back, only they didn't. They kept going, because they were holding on to something… That there's some good in this world, Mr. Frodo… and it's worth fighting for."

Even after the deepest of losses, your happiness and well-being are also worth fighting for. I share my experience with the hope it gives you strength, to keep holding on, until the day you're standing in *your own Glorious* life.

As you read my grief origin story, you'll likely notice ways in which your loss is similar and how it's different. Perhaps you'll empathize with my sadness but see my happiness as unattainable.

You may be shaking your head now, thinking, *"No. There's no possible way I can ever be truly happy again."* I understand because I used to think that, too. But I was wrong. And I'm glad to admit it, so you can believe what Sam said to Mr. Frodo is true: the darkness will pass, a new day will come, and when the sun comes, it will shine out the clearer.

Origins

I got the call shortly after eating my Lean Cuisine lunch on Tuesday, June 3, 2003. My intercom buzzed and the receptionist said, "Your babysitter on line two."

I felt a moment of fear. In the recesses of my mind, I suspected this was not the ordinary phone call in which the sitter would ask me to bring more diapers. But I shoved down whatever was trying to bubble up and went with my default approach… assume everything is fine until circumstances prove otherwise.

I picked up the phone calmly, pretending those were not the final seconds separating the before and the after.

Melanie screamed, "Jackson went down for a nap, and he was

asleep a long time. Mom checked on him and he wasn't breathing. We called 911, and they're here now."

I don't know what I said, something along the lines of: "*What???* Is he breathing now? Did they revive him? What's happening?"

Melanie said, "I don't know, they're outside in the ambulance. I don't understand. He was having a great day. Everything was normal." She rambled on far too long, while I sat staring at the beige wallpaper, silently begging God to save my baby. Every second brought me closer to the truth. A few minutes later she said the ambulance left, headed to the children's hospital.

I raced to the emergency room and got the news I knew was coming. My baby didn't start breathing again. He was gone.

Never could I have imagined the crushing pain that took over my life that day, nor the length of time it would last. Because I'm a pragmatic, problem-solving person, I wasted no time trying to figure out 1) how to survive and 2) how to be happy again someday. I read books. I journaled. I joined a SIDS (Sudden Infant Death Syndrome) support group. I also went back to work three days after the funeral because I couldn't sit home and cry 24/7.

My Epic Attempt to Control Grief

Back when I worked in a cubicle (circa 1993), there was a bullet-shaped mahogany desk dividing the space between my cubemate, Mike, and me. He was a great guy, but he was *loud*. He frequently put headphones on and jammed out to his tunes, thumping on the desk, bobbing his head, channeling Don Henley, and singing, "Welcome to the Hotel California."

Co-workers across the aisle would stand and peer over their navy blue, cushion-covered, cubicle walls and hiss, "Mike, *be quiet!*" Then they'd look at me with the question in their eyes, *How can you stand him?*

I'd look up from my computer, confused, asking, "What?" Their bulging eyes and irritated sideways glances at Mike clued me in. I'd say, "Oh, him… I just tune him out."

Suffice it to say, one thing I do really well is focus on the task at hand and ignore everything else. This "ability" keeps my productivity high. But ignoring everything is a mixed bag when it comes to grief. On one hand, my focus-power allowed me to return to my demanding job a week after Jackson's death and raise my two subsequent children pretty much single-handedly (both before and after the divorce).

On the other hand, focusing entirely on my responsibilities meant I didn't deal with my grief. I compartmentalized it. I tried to control my anguish by shoving it into a box and slamming the lid shut. I went to work. I took care of my kids. *I didn't have time to pee, or eat, much less grieve.*

Fast forward ten years to 2013, when I joined a women's Bible study. This was my first sustained social interaction since Jackson's death. Each week I listened to the ladies vulnerably share their painful stories, right there in front of 20+ other ladies. *Wow.* I realized how far I'd distanced myself from my friends and family, for *ten years!* *(Insert Homer Simpson forehead slap: D'oh!)*

I tried to control my anguish by shoving it into a box and slamming the lid shut.

Why did I avoid connecting with people for so many years? Largely, because no one wants to have a conversation about your child's death. On too many occasions, when I'd tell someone about Jackson, thick tension arose and swirled between us. And the silence was thunderous. The death of a child is too terrifying to contemplate, much less discuss in polite society, so most people had a sudden need to use the restroom and made a quick exit. I learned to keep my story to myself.

Thankfully, there was one exception, an online support group for SIDS moms. I found tremendous relief in this group where I could share the whole truth about my grief and pain. But I couldn't be so disturbingly honest with my mom or sisters or anyone else who loved me because I knew how badly it would hurt them. Plus, they couldn't truly understand. (*Insert another forehead slap: D'oh!*) I didn't know at the time how wrong I was... because *people don't have to understand your loss 100% to be there for you.* I get that *now.*

But back then, I concentrated on my responsibilities and pretended to be okay. And it's not like I didn't deal with my grief *at all.* I did what I could under the circumstances. I wrote in my journal, read a lot of books, and leaned on my SIDS group. But with hindsight I see that I was using my focus-power not only to survive, but to control, and maybe even outrun my pain.

Waiting for Someday

A few months after Jackson died, my sister Kay emailed:

> I have been praying for you. I wish so much that there was something more that I could do. I worry about you all the time. Please take care of yourself and do everything you can to get through this impossibly difficult time.

I replied:

> I wish I could tell you not to worry, but I know the only way you would stop worrying is if I told you I felt fine and I'm not there yet. So I guess we both have to keep doing what we're doing.
>
> I'm doing the best I can and based on some of the emails from my support group, I'm actually doing a lot better than most. So there's one positive thing I can say. But bottom line, it's like you said, this is just an "impossibly difficult time." I'm trying to keep my eye on someday.
>
> I believe someday I'll feel good again even though the short term looks pretty crappy. I can say from the bottom of my heart that Jackson was an incredible gift and he made me

the happiest mommy in the world and I wouldn't trade that for anything, not even to avoid the pain I feel now.

So with that seed of gratitude and a focus on someday, I shut my grief and pain in a box. The feelings tried to come out, but I didn't have the time or energy, so I kept the lid closed. I sat on that box like one of those old crank toys with a bouncing clown head and an accordion neck that pops out, causing you to startle in fear.

A decade later, I'd say I was doing alright, happy and content for the most part. Yet, the damn box (where my grief was held in captivity) was intent on opening to free the rightful feelings demanding attention. I was indignant. *Why let the clown pop out now?* I squeezed and pressed against the swelling sides of the box and even bounced on top like you would an overstuffed suitcase for a ski trip to Lake Tahoe. But it wouldn't stay shut.

After ten years of running, the jig was up. I began having sporadic fainting spells. A sudden hot flash would come over me, quickly followed by nausea. Then my vision would narrow, like at the end of an old cartoon, with the black and white kaleidoscope closing in. At that point I would just plop down on the nearest chair or the floor to avoid falling.

I couldn't be fainting in meetings, or making dinner, or God forbid when driving the kids to school. I had to do *something* to fix this. So, I consulted several doctors, went to physical therapy, and solved the fainting problem.

And you know what I did after that? I went right back to my old ways: focus, focus, focus. I told myself, *I'm fine, I'm fine, I'm fine.* I kept doing my job, taking care of others, letting no one take care of me… not even myself. Why didn't I learn anything from my health scare?

Holding on to False Beliefs

I didn't realize my unresolved pain, the deep wound I buried, handicapped me with false beliefs. Have you ever put the brakes on healing by thinking things like this:

➤ Life is good… *good enough.*

➤ Lingering sadness and pain are just a fact of life after loss, and there's nothing to be done for this kind of ache in my soul.

I once heard Rick Warren say that Satan uses not only our weakness against us but more so, our biggest strengths (the Carey Nieuwhof Leadership Podcast Episode 467). *Ain't that the truth.* I'm incredibly independent, which in many areas of life is a good thing. But my independent nature is extreme to the point of being obnoxious. With few exceptions, I didn't open up to people, share my story, or ask anyone for help; doing so would've put my fundamental nature and my false beliefs to the test. Besides, I thought I'd already done everything that could be done.

I didn't realize my unresolved pain, the deep wound I buried, handicapped me with false beliefs.

I kept my tormented feelings in that box for another seven years. And they might still be there today *except*, thankfully, there's one thing stronger than my desire to do all things on my own… my desire to help people in need. (I know, the irony of me saying "No, No, I don't need help. But really, you should let me help you.")

Wonder what *finally* got me to open the box after so many years? Are you ready? *Boing!* It wasn't about me. I took that big step so I could help someone else. A coaching client asked me for help coping with the loss of her husband. Even though I'd experienced grief, understood grief, and was well-read on the topic, I found my tools weren't enough to provide a transformative experience for her.

Accidental Transformation

In 2020, I signed up to be certified as a Grief Recovery Method® Specialist. As part of the certification process, you work through your life history of losses and drill down into one specific loss. I chose to work on the loss of my dad, which I thought would be easier than talking about the death of my baby, Jackson.

You don't know this about me yet, but I'm not a crier, at *all*. I don't like sharing or showing my feelings. So, I thought I stood a good chance of not breaking down crying in front of a room full of strangers. *Wrong.* I started crying in the first thirty minutes on the first day during introductions, when we went around the room and gave our name and shared the loss/losses that brought us there. I proceeded to cry more in the next two days than I had in *years*.

Much of the work in the program is done with a partner, and mine was EdRicardo, a beautiful human with surprisingly mild mannerisms and a gentle spirit, which contrasted with his tall, strong build. He had soulful milk chocolate brown eyes. We sat facing each other in black metal chairs with ivory cushioned seats, a box of Kleenex on the floor between us. Clusters of other groups were spread out around the room.

I leaned toward him and shared every loss and major challenge I'd experienced in life. I told him about childhood heartaches, failed relationships and marriages, raising a child with a developmental disorder, the death of my father, and the death of my son. We cried, tears pouring from our eyes in silent sobs, snot running out of our noses to join the tears and journey across our lips, down our chins, dropping off, and splashing in our laps.

Those tears were sacred tears of holy healing... ushering in the miracles of profound joy and whispers of peace.

My miracle moment happened in a room full of strangers, where I did something I didn't think I needed to do. I shared my story. *All* of it. With another human there to witness and affirm the significance of my suffering. And I cried, a lot, releasing and letting go of a lifetime of heartache and pain.

Before my grief training, I had no idea how much loss and trauma people experience in life without ever dealing with it. We just try to recover as quickly as possible because that's what people expect.

Don't make the mistake I did. Don't try to control grief by shoving it into a box. Don't hide from your family, friends, and the world for seventeen years. It won't work anyway. The weight of unresolved pain will be your constant companion. Only pain that is felt, honored, and witnessed can be healed and resolved. Once it's resolved, it can be let go. That's how we transform grief.

For years I tried to get by with sharing pieces of my story now and then, but that wasn't enough. I hadn't done the deeper excavation… to uncover a lifetime of losses that had been ignored, remained unhealed, and continued to cause emotional and physical pain.

Through my training I found, though admittedly it was by accident, a safe space with the time and structure to face those old wounds and tend to them at last.

I emptied my box of past hurts by the end of the program, and my body felt lighter. My chest was open, full of air and excited anticipation instead of waiting for the next heart-shattering phone call. My shoulders stood tall, instead of sagging and hunching over, drawing my heart deep inside to hide and protect it.

When I imagined what the future might hold, I felt practically giddy. The walls I unknowingly erected between the world and me came down. Not to mention that my sorrow was gone, leaving me with a box full of *love* and happy memories. (You'll find the full account of how I transformed my grief in Chapters 10 and 11).

Only pain that is felt, honored, and witnessed can be healed and resolved. Once it's resolved, it can be let go.

Conclusion

I know facing the pain is scary. You just read how I held back for years and avoided my grief at all costs. Maybe your journey has been similar. You've shared to some extent, but for the most part, you've been carrying the mountainous weight of grief on your own two sagging shoulders.

Transforming your grief into a life of joy and purpose involves letting your resistance down and sharing the burden of loss… not only the loss that feels the heaviest but all the other losses that have been neglected and thus continue to cause pain. Feeling the pain, as frightening as it is, turns out to be the very key to letting it go.

And while I once feared that releasing the pain would also mean letting go of my lost loved ones, that wasn't the case. In fact, my connection to Jackson and my dad felt stronger than ever because I'd learned this truth:

Grief isn't a life sentence or a punishment. It's the sacred honoring of love. Grief and love are bound, in a covenant that endures beyond death, beyond explanation, beyond understanding.

To fully embrace this truth, we first have to dismantle the mistaken beliefs about grief that box in your healing potential.

TWO

MISTAKEN BELIEFS ABOUT GRIEF (YOU'RE NOT CRAZY: SOCIETY IS JUST CLUELESS)

One day shortly after my return to work, a vendor stopped by with breakfast tacos. He paused at the door to my office, afraid to come in or maybe preparing what to say. He leaned across my desk and handed me my favorite, bacon and egg. Then he retreated to the safety of the doorway before offering condolences.

During our stilted conversation, he said, "Everything happens for a reason." He seemed to think I would find that comforting but alas, I did not. The fact that there might be some reason why my son died didn't ease my pain in the slightest.

Comments like this show up often in grief. People believe they're helping when in fact, they make you feel worse.

I call these comments *"mistakements"* (a combination of *mistake* + *statement*). Such statements are well-intended but mistaken nonetheless, usually born out of a cliché or a misbelief about grief.

My vendor friend didn't mean to be hurtful. He was just repeating a cliché he'd heard. So I smiled and thanked him for the taco.

Unfortunately, he followed up his first *"mistakement"* with another, suggesting that maybe Jackson living only three months was a *good thing* because I hadn't had much time to bond with him. And therefore I would be able to 'get over it' easier. At that, my face turned as red as the Picante sauce on my taco.

I paused and breathed, knowing his intention wasn't to minimize my loss. He simply had no idea how to communicate about death and grief.

There were times I didn't know what to say either. When someone asked a simple, everyday question like, "How many children do you have?" I'd answer honestly, "Three, but one is dead now." Obviously, that never went over well. It was like dropping an emotional bomb on an unsuspecting person, and unsurprisingly, their response would be to leave as fast as possible.

So, I learned to listen. Which incidentally, is quite ironic because throughout childhood, all I ever did was talk. Grief changed that about me. I became a master at deflecting personal questions and hiding my feelings.

I thought my story didn't need to be told, not to most people anyway. I learned to fly under the radar and have one-way relationships, listening but not sharing. I hid myself for twenty years.

Listening to others is important, but a balance of sharing and listening is needed for emotional well-being. A 2022 study on loneliness conducted by the Society for Personality and Social Psychology finds that not sharing your stories and feelings leads to an increased sense of isolation and disconnection.[2]

While I coped with grief through working and giving, changing my pattern of isolation has been a struggle. I knew I had to open up to have functioning relationships again. And that left me wondering: *Why, when talking about grief is so beneficial, does it have to feel so frightening, almost unbearable?* My answer boils down to society's pervasive misconceptions about grief.

Most people don't get grief until they go through it. They think the misbeliefs and clichés are true and accidentally say hurtful, unsupportive things. Only when they find themselves on their knees in a hospital bathroom, crying and asking, *"Why God?"* do they begin to realize everything they thought about grief was totally wrong.

In this chapter, I break down six of the most common mistaken beliefs about grief and contrast them with the truth. Armed with this information, you'll be better prepared to handle *"mistakements."* More importantly, you'll be better equipped to gently guide people to listen and allow you to authentically tell your grief story, instead of feeling like you have to avoid it.

As you review the list of mistaken beliefs, you may be reminded of especially hurtful *"mistakements"* people made that you still find upsetting. You may want to grab a journal and write about the hurtful comments and misbeliefs that frustrate or trigger you the most. This isn't an exhaustive list so please feel free to note and write about any additional mistaken beliefs that come up for you.

Misbelief #1: Grief is Only About Death

When I mention "grief" to someone who's going through a divorce or whose child moved away to college, oftentimes their knee-jerk reaction is, "Oh, this isn't grief. It's not like anyone died."

Most people believe grief is what you feel when someone dies. And while that is true, death is not the only kind of loss that wounds us. As John James and Russell Friedman explain in *The Grief Recovery Handbook*, grief is "the normal and natural reaction to loss of any kind."

Megan Devine echoes and expands this truth in *It's OK That You're Not OK*:

> "Everyone carries grief—from the everyday losses to the bigger, life-altering ones. Because we don't talk about grief in our culture, we have personal and global backlogs of unheard and unspoken grief."

A big reason people carry unspoken grief is the mistaken belief that we can only grieve when there's a death. Yet grief shows up on many more occasions than we realize. According to *The Grief Recovery Handbook*, there are more than 40 causes of grief, only two of which involve death: the loss of beloved humans and pets. The rest arise from life's challenges and transitions. Here are just a few:

- Divorce (or the end of any significant relationship)
- Moving (loss of familiar home, community, friends)
- Unemployment (loss of stability, security, self-confidence)
- Major health changes (losing functional ability and routines being completely altered)
- Menopause (hormone and body changes, plus the end of childbearing years)
- Empty nest (loss of nuclear family parenting roles, loss of your child's presence)
- Retirement (loss of routine, co-workers, purpose, status)

How many of these types of losses have you experienced? Very likely, you've felt grief many times in life due to losses caused by major life transitions. As I mentioned in the Introduction, I call this *life-transition grief*.

You may not have realized this and wondered, *What the hell is wrong with me?* Feeling lost, confused, lethargic, depressed, anxious, detached, or aimless might've felt silly or overly dramatic because society doesn't teach us we experience loss (and therefore grief) many times in life, and these losses have nothing to do with someone dying. Which leads us to the next mistaken belief.

Misbelief #2: Big Feelings Are Acceptable Only If Someone Dies

Society often sends the message that losses unrelated to death don't really count… because a person can simply think and DO their way back to normal. Society tends to downplay painful feelings and imply something's wrong with people if they don't bounce back from life challenges *fast*.

Minimizing attitudes are often communicated in maxims like:

➢ *Life goes on...*
➢ *What doesn't kill you makes you stronger...*
➢ *Fake it until you make it...*

These slogans treat emotional upheavals like something grievers can ignore their way through, like an Olympic runner who "feels the burn" and keeps running. A better comparison is the grief professional athletes feel when they retire, losing their identity and purpose. Major life transitions bring real and valid feelings of grief, even when no one has died.

Perhaps the most insidious way we minimize grief is to use God to explain it away. Grievers don't need explanations or faith-based platitudes. They need space to be devastated without feeling spiritually corrected.

Major life transitions bring real and valid feelings of grief, even when no one has died.

I cringe when people say, *"God never gives you more than you can handle."* This comes from I Corinthians 10:13, about God not giving us more "temptation" than we can handle. I've heard pastors apply this generally to the trials and tribulations of life, but even if true, would that have been comforting to Job in his darkest hour?

Paul writes in Romans 12:15, "Rejoice with those who rejoice; weep with those who weep." *If anyone wants to apply scripture to grief, I suggest starting there.*

Misbelief #3: Grievers Eventually "Get Over It" and "Go Back to Normal"

I went back to work a week after my son died. It probably sounds bizarre, but staying busy is how I was raised and the only thing I knew to do.

A month or two after I was back at work, long after the initial days of hugs and tears, the owner's mom, Ruth, stopped by. I hadn't seen her since before my pregnancy. So, I was surprised when, the minute I came around the wood-paneled corner, she dropped her quilted handbag and grabbed me into a tight hug.

She didn't say a word. She just held her arms around me for a long time. When we pulled apart, she looked at me with tears in her eyes. I didn't know that she, too, had lost a child. Her daughter, Cathy, died in 1956, a whopping forty-nine years prior.

At the time, I didn't understand why Ruth's sympathy was so intense. We weren't *that* close. Now I realize, my loss triggered memories of her loss. And, she knew something I hadn't yet learned: a mother never stops loving or missing her child, not after five years, not after fifty. She cried remembering her own pain and in sympathy for me. She knew the trajectory of my life was forever changed.

Most people aren't like Ruth. Without the experience of profound loss, they have the unrealistic expectation that you'll be "back to normal" after a year or two. They don't understand that a traumatic experience fundamentally changes you. *You do not go back to your old self.* I will forever be a mother of three, two living, one not.

In addition to grief altering our fundamental being, it isn't "over" at a specific time like a curfew or last call. Ridiculous statements like, "It's been two years; I thought you'd be over it by now" leave us feeling like we're doing something wrong.

Grief isn't like a too-tight pair of pants you can strip off at the end of a long day and breathe easy. Grief is something we must learn to live with, not a temporary inconvenience.

People blind to the reality of grief can't understand the depth or duration of your pain. They mean well, but they don't know what they don't know. *They really believe "time heals all wounds."* And while it's not our job to educate everyone, we also don't have to accept their misbeliefs as truth.

Grief expert David Kessler explains the reality of grief's timeline like this:

Question: How long will I grieve?

Answer: How long will they be dead?

Misbelief #4: A Loss Can Be Replaced

This mistaken belief shows up in comments like these:

> ➤ *You're young. You can re-marry.*
> ➤ *You can have more children.*
> ➤ *Let's get you a new dog.*

Grief doesn't work that way. You can't simply get a new thing to erase the pain you feel over the thing you lost.

Particularly with pet loss, people think replacing the loss is a perfectly reasonable suggestion, "Get a new dog. That will make you feel better!" *Not likely.*

My hairdresser and dear friend Hannah lost her beloved Pomeranian, Isis, last year and was devastated. She told me one day as she worked her magic, covering my head in shiny tin foil squares, that she couldn't talk to anyone else about Isis. Every time she tried, she wound up crying, and then people acted weird and uncomfortable. Like something was wrong with her for crying over a dog.

They didn't understand. Isis wasn't just a pet. She was Hannah's constant companion, her "ride or die" who had been by her side through every major life transition… marriage, childbirth, divorce, starting over, surgeries and recoveries, remarriage. Isis was there for every heartbreak and every comeback. This was a love second only to that of her husband and son.

Suggesting a new dog could trot in and make everything better is insensitive and, frankly, stupid.

If you've lost a pet and people suggest you get a new pet or that you should be "over it" within a short period of time, *do not let them minimize your loss.* Profound sadness over the loss of a cherished pet is perfectly natural. Because the source of deep grief is deep love.

Grief demands to be felt, not fixed.

Misbelief #5: If Grievers Look at the Silver Lining, They Won't Feel Bad Anymore

Do you know what statements like these have in common?

> ➤ *At least they're not suffering anymore.*
> ➤ *He lived a good, long life.*
> ➤ *Now you can live your own life instead of being a caregiver.*
> ➤ *Be glad for the time you had together.*
> ➤ *You still have your health, a nice home, a good job, and a 401k plan.*

Statements like these suggest grievers shouldn't feel bad because of the so-called silver lining.

People say things like this hoping to make grievers feel better. But it doesn't work. Because logical facts and observations can't resolve an emotional crisis. If these ideas worked, then we could say, "Oh, good point. I feel better already." *And we would actually feel better.*

But grief isn't a math problem. You can't solve it. Grief demands to be felt, not fixed.

Unfortunately, *"mistakements"* such as those above often leave grievers feeling frustrated and even more upset. The mistaken belief that silver linings are healing agents can lead grievers to blame themselves for feeling pain instead of shutting it down with logic or gratitude.

If we could, a griever in agony might say: *Thank you for trying.*

But this situation can't be made better by "looking on the bright side." Please keep being here for me even if it's awkward. I'm having a hard time forming thoughts and sentences. I need you. I would tell you exactly what to do for me if I knew how.

Loss causes tremendous pain. Our hearts don't think; they feel. **Grievers need to be encouraged to honor their emotions, not handed logical reasons to dismiss them.**

As grief expert David Kessler says, "You can't heal it if you don't feel it." A griever's pain must be affirmed, not treated like a riddle that just needs the right answer.

Rationalizing with someone who's heartbroken is a trifecta of wrong:

➤ Insensitive
➤ Inappropriate
➤ Ineffective

Gratitude and the ability to focus on the positive only come later… after the pain has been felt, not bypassed.

Misbelief #6: Grief is a Process that Happens in Five Stages and Then It's Over

"How long until you feel better?" my sister asked, a few months after Jackson's death. She wanted to have some idea of what to expect. She also wanted to know when it was time to become concerned about me, should I not make the anticipated progress.

My therapist's answer was long and clinical but basically, we could expect I'd be feeling "consistently better" after approximately a year. This answer seems to be a common rule of thumb based on… *absolute nonsense.* After one year, there's still *tremendous* pain, turmoil, crying, anguish, and all the things that coincide with deep grief.

You may be wondering, "Why don't people, especially therapists, understand this?" Well, the answer begins with the long-held theory that grief has five stages, based on Elisabeth Kübler-Ross's study of patients facing terminal illness. She published her findings in *On Death and Dying* in 1969.

Kübler-Ross identified the different feelings and stages a *terminally ill person* goes through as they come to terms with their own impending death: Denial, Anger, Bargaining, Depression, and Acceptance. **These stages document the grief of a dying person. They were never intended to describe the grief process of someone mourning the death of another person.**

Unfortunately, society misapplied the Five Stages to all forms of grief even though that's not what the author intended.

In addition, society came to presume that once a griever moved through the five stages, the work of grief would be done. They would have healed, accepted their loss, and moved on with their life, leaving grief behind.

I find this to be the most regrettable aspect of the five stages being universally misunderstood: the implication that grief ends when you reach the "final" stage of acceptance. It's one reason I created my own model of grief transformation (which we'll get to in the next chapter).

The false idea that there's an end to grief gives non-grievers unrealistic expectations of how people in grief "should" behave. And that creates pressure on grievers. Pressure to be okay. Pressure to stop talking about it. Pressure to act like their world didn't implode.

Grievers, faced with an overwhelming majority of people (including therapists) who can't fathom their continued pain, are left to manage on their own. I know this firsthand.

Nearly two decades after Jackson died, I was still wrestling with the world's expectation that I should be "over it" by now. I was still searching for confirmation of what I knew deep down: Accepting my loss didn't mean I was "over it." Here's what I wrote in my journal.

May 11, 2021

I started reading a new book last night... Jeffery Olsen's memoir. His wife and youngest son died in a tragic car accident.

When I got up for a bathroom break, I wondered, "Why do I keep reading books about grief and loss? I've achieved a certain level of healing and happiness. Why am I still drawn to these stories?"

After letting my thoughts ping-pong around, I landed on a reason: I like to read other people's grief stories because they validate what I've found to be true... you never get over it. I feel better reading stories about people claiming their right to love forever and never "move on."

What's truly ironic is, those people who are concerned about whether I've moved on, whether I'm handling my grief in a healthy way, they don't understand. The most unhealthy thing that could happen is if I gave in to the pressure to get over it and I stopped talking about my son and stopped honoring his special dates.

I'm doing what's healthy by continuing my relationship with my dead son. He's with me, always. He's my inspiration for so many things! He's not forgotten. He's still deeply loved. My life is forever changed by him and the lives of many others have been changed by him through me.

A huge portion of the purpose I feel comes from him. And I'm so blessed to be his mom and to honor the love we share. Yes, present tense, share. The love is not in the past. It's in the present and in the future. It is now. It is always.

Conclusion

Here are some truths about grief you can rely on instead of all the nonsense surrounding the Mistaken Beliefs society holds:

1. Grief isn't only about death.
2. Feeling tremendous sadness over the loss of a job, a home, or a relationship isn't weird or wrong.
3. Grief evolves, but it doesn't end.
4. When you feel defeated, lost, and depressed after a loss, it's natural. And you can't be made to feel better by getting a "new" thing.
5. You will feel sad after loss, and no amount of logic will change that. Others may not understand, but you don't need their understanding or permission to honor your own feelings.
6. Grief is a messy, unpredictable, uniquely individual process that doesn't happen in stages.

Don't accept unrealistic timelines and unfair expectations of a grief-illiterate culture.

You're not broken. You're not too much. You're grieving. And you need to do it your way.

THREE

Forget the Five Stages: A Grief Model that Finally Makes Sense

Now that we've covered what grief is *not*, let's talk about what it's really like when you're in it.

You may feel lost, stuck, and alone… still sad and feeling like you shouldn't be because no one understands. If so, as I said earlier, there's nothing wrong with you. *You're not crazy.* Grievers often worry they might be crazy because society has grief all wrong.

Despite what society has told you, you're not grieving wrong or for too long. Maybe you've just never been shown that it's possible to move forward after loss *without* moving on.

Wait a minute. *Without moving on?*

Now, you may wonder, "Are you sure, Jennifer? I just don't see how that could be true."

Yes, I'm sure. You can move forward with your life *and* maintain your connection with your loved one. I say this twenty years into my grief journey. As you read in my journal entry from the last chapter, I'm never going to "get over it," and that is as it should be.

I still cry when I hear Rod Stewart sing, "Have I told you lately that I love you?" It gets me every time. And a few months ago, I was watching *Top Gun,* when the medics insisted Maverick let go of Goose's dead body. I couldn't stop the flood of tears as they said, "Sir, you have to let him go now." Why wouldn't they let Maverick hold him a little longer?

My tears don't mean I'm depressed or in denial. They mean I loved. And I still do.

That scene took me back in time, when the hospital nurses showed my family into the Cloud Room. They said, "You can stay with him as long as you'd like." It felt like only an hour later, when they returned saying, "We're so sorry but the medical examiner is here. He can't wait. We have to take your son now." It was such a cruel blow… the first of many injuries stacked on top of the devastating injury of losing my baby.

Though I still have moments when a painful memory drops in without warning, like that night watching *Top Gun,* my tears don't mean I'm depressed or in denial. They mean I loved. And I still do.

The Trouble with Labels

Bursts of sadness are not a sign of unhealthy ongoing attachment, mental illness, or Prolonged Grief Disorder (PGD). PGD is a new diagnosis of the American Psychiatric Association (APA) published in its 2022 *Diagnostic and Statistical Manual of Mental Disorders*. This so-called disorder describes adults severely mourning a loss after one year as mentally ill.[3]

Labeling people who mourn a loss for longer than a year as mentally ill… now *that* is crazy!

Grief expert Alan Wolfelt rebuts the PGD diagnosis saying:

"First, the term 'prolonged' implies that one year is sufficient for deep grief, but this is an arbitrary cutoff. The truth is that there is no timetable to healing in grief. Besides, working toward reconciling grief waits on welcome, not on time. And second, the term 'disorder' shames grievers at the very moment when what they need most is affirmation, empathy, and compassion."[4]

Mr. Wolfelt is right. The identification of Prolonged Grief Disorder sets up unrealistic expectations and further harms grievers.

Five Stages that Don't Fit

The APA's misconception that grief has a regular timetable is not surprising considering the 6th Misbelief of Grief discussed in the last chapter—about those pesky 5 Stages of Grief (Denial, Anger, Bargaining, Depression, and Acceptance).

As a reminder, Elisabeth Kübler-Ross originally created the stages to describe the experience of *terminally ill patients* facing their own death, not those grieving someone else's death.

Here's an illustration of how the five stages fall short and fit no griever's actual experience. Imagine a garden designed to grow succulents, but you plant roses instead. When the roses don't bloom, you wonder, "What's wrong with these flowers?" The problem isn't the roses. A garden built for succulents will not bring forth flourishing pink roses. That doesn't mean there's something wrong with the roses. Succulents and roses have totally different growing cycles and needs for sunlight, water, and soil.

That's how it is with grief. The grief of the dying is not the same as the grief of those left behind. And even among the grieving, no two hearts heal the same way. What comforts one may not comfort another.

A garden created to nurture one person's grief won't mend someone else's broken heart.

You're Not Broken: The Model Was

My Grief Transformation Model turns the Five Stages theory on its ear. I've struggled with those stages for years… because they leave grievers second-guessing themselves when pain doesn't show up (or go away) according to plan.

Society still clings to the idea that grief should unfold in five predictable steps… like going through airport security:

1. Get in line
2. Show your boarding pass and ID
3. Remove your belt and the contents of your pockets
4. Get scanned
5. Collect your belongings from the gray bins and head to Starbucks

But grief doesn't follow directions or offer that kind of order. It defies the straight path and moves like the tide, swelling, receding, and rushing back. Its motion is fluid and overlapping, always returning, never ending.

I suspect the idea of "never ending" may cause you to have mixed feelings. On one hand, it makes sense, because love doesn't end. On the other hand, you can't help but wonder, "What about the *pain…* does it ever end?"

Here's what I've learned. *No, the pain doesn't completely end.* But there is hope to hold onto: *You can let go of pain without letting go of your person.*

I live a joyful, meaningful life. But not because I finally healed enough to "accept" my loss. I didn't wake up one magical morning and think, "You know what, I'm totally fine that Jackson isn't here. I don't even miss him anymore." That day will never come because love never ends. And so, neither does grief.

That's why I said earlier, you don't have to move on from grief. It's going to be with you. And you can move forward *with* the grief.

Over time, pain does soften. But love… it stays and grows stronger.

Love becomes your comfort. Your companion. A balm to your soul.

So, would you like to feel the pain *less* and the love *more*? My Grief Transformation Model shows you what the process looks like and what you can look forward to in the future. No stages included.

Grief Transformation Model: 6 G's From Gutted to Glorious

I created a framework to help grievers find sparks of hope and sigh in relief. I call it the *Grief Transformation Model: 6 G's from Gutted to Glorious.*

Now please don't check out because feeling Glorious sounds like crazy-talk. I understand why you might think that way. In the early years of my journey, the idea of Glorious would have triggered an immediate protest: *"Yeah right... when pigs fly."*

But I promise you Glorious is attainable, and I wouldn't lie about such a thing. Actually, I wouldn't lie about anything. I'm a terrible liar. I'm like a deer in the headlights if I even contemplate uttering a small fib. But as I was saying, if you put in the energy and effort required to heal, the moment can arrive when you reach that glorious state and discover:

- *The 10-ton weight of pain has lifted.*
- *Your desire to live a happy life no longer causes guilt or feelings of betrayal.*
- *You've left the really dark places behind and you look forward to what lies ahead.*
- *Memories of your loved one no longer feel like a knife to the heart. Instead they're your greatest comfort.*

And when you arrive to the joy that feels out of reach today, you'll be so thankful to yourself for finding a tool that actually helps you be fully present and participating in life again after your loss.

In the meantime, you don't have to agree that Glorious is possible. Even if you have lingering thoughts like these:

- *I'm afraid I'll be stuck forever in this heavy stage of grieving.*
- *It's been 3 years, and I still don't want to get out of bed or face the world.*
- *I can barely get through the moment, let alone think about the future.*

You're in the right place. Put Glorious to the side. Let's get you feeling better than Gutted or Grinding for starters.

Once you decide you want the kind of healing and growth my Grief Transformation model illustrates, you'll make more progress than you can imagine. How do I know? Because I had those same thoughts once upon a time.

I thought I'd never be whole again. But I'm glad to say, I was wrong.

And you should know, that's saying something. I don't admit to being wrong often, not because of ego, but because I don't take a big stand if I'm not sure. My family knows: don't bet Mom unless you're ready to lose. (Ask my former husband about the time I won $1,000 when he swore his dad's eyes were brown. They were sky blue. Think Paul Newman and Zac Efron, the kind of unforgettable that made my wager a sure thing.)

So when I say I was wrong about healing, it's a big announcement. And I say it with joy. Because you need to know: whole *is* possible.

That's why I turned my model into this graphic to show you how your life after loss journey can blossom into grief transformation.

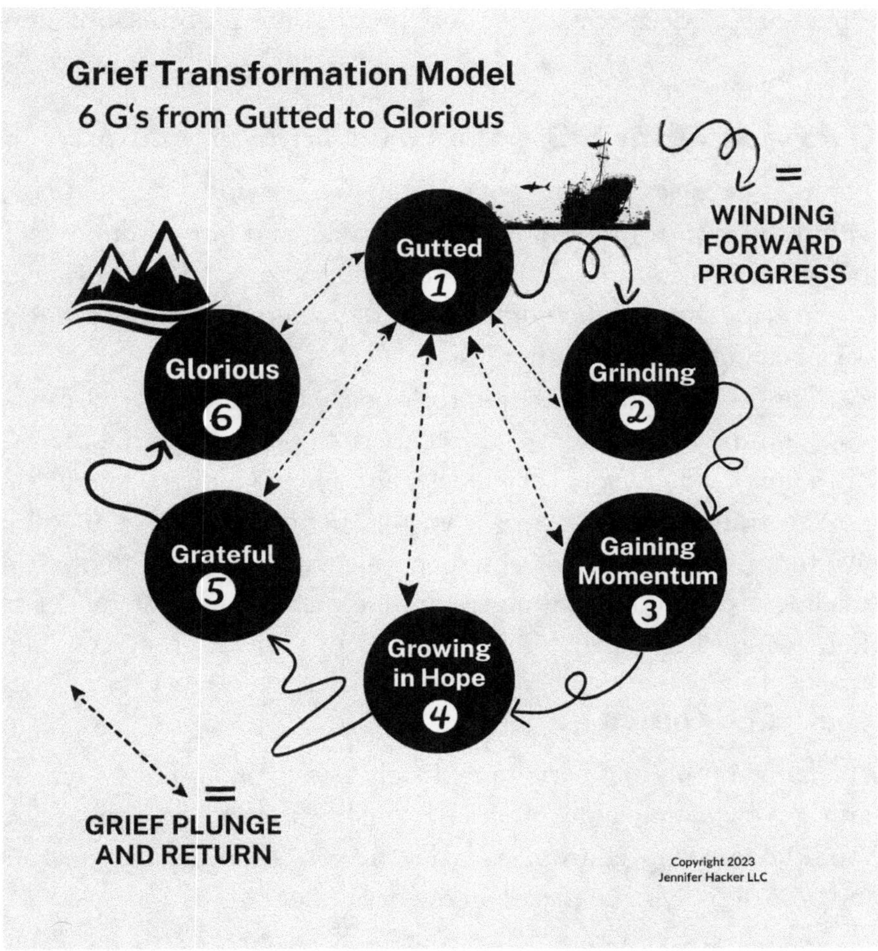

What Do You Notice?

Many clients immediately see this model is much more intuitive than the Five Stages. They notice the perforated lines, the loops, and the winding curves. This isn't a climb up a ladder. Instead, it reflects the reality of grief: twists, setbacks, and forward surges, all within an ocean of emotions. Riptides may pull you under, but you resurface and continue your healing journey.

You progress on a winding, non-linear path. In this way, the 6 G's of Grief Transformation is much more accurate to the actual experience of deep loss, emotional progression, and the evolution of grief.

Overview of the 6 G's of a Grief Transformation

The 6 G's *are not* steps or phases. They're periods, or gradations, within the grief transformation. You change and move from one G to another in a continuous, unorderly, and *overlapping* fashion. The 6 G's describe the evolution of grief and the different ways life can feel as you change and grow after loss.

The first period, Gutted, is rock bottom, where you feel like a wreck on the ocean floor. The sixth period, Glorious, is the mountain summit, where you feel whole again, shining with joy and light.

You transform and move from one period to another in your own time. There's no right or wrong way, and there's no "standard" timeline. Every individual moves around and through the model at their own pace.

The 1st G: Gutted

The name of this first period practically says it all. You're overcome with sorrow, barely able (oftentimes unable) to manage basic tasks. You're so far removed from everyday life you're like a ship, wrecked and destroyed, lying in pieces on the ocean floor.

Most likely, you experience four of Kübler-Ross's stages all at once: denial, bargaining, anger, and depression.

The effects of this period surface in every part of you… physically, mentally, emotionally, spiritually. Common experiences during Gutted include:

- Physical symptoms of grief: nausea, stomach cramps, headaches, heart palpitations, insomnia, and crushing fatigue.
- "Grief brain" or "brain fog"—when concentrating, thinking, or making simple decisions feels nearly impossible.
- A sense of detachment, as if you're watching the world from outside your body, either from above or through thick glass.

- A complete lack of interest in anything that used to matter.

Most people grounded enough to read this book (or any book) are likely no longer fully in this period but you remember it vividly. And when certain dates, holidays, or unexpected memories arise, even in later periods of grief transformation, you can be plunged right back into Gutted and feel the sting of pain while gasping for air.

The 2nd G: Grinding

You're persevering and functioning in the second period for the most part, but EVERYTHING requires a Grinding effort:

- Every task, every responsibility, feels like endless unwanted chores.
- Depression and anger linger and hover close.
- You may not cry every day but the tears are there, just under the surface, always threatening to break through at any moment.
- Things you once handled with ease now feel overwhelming, even frightening.
- Avoiding people and conversations is a regular coping mechanism.

You're teaching yourself to live without your loved one in the world, and this requires tiny steps that may feel like running in quicksand. The only way through this period of grief is through it as you build consistent, life-affirming habits that eventually create your healing momentum.

The 3rd G: Gaining Momentum

In the third period, you're Gaining Momentum. Loss doesn't dominate your every thought and action. You still feel sad, moody, and irritable oftentimes, but other times you're able to enjoy "normal" things like dinner with a friend, watching TV, or running errands.

- You try your best to be in the present moment and actually succeed a lot of the time.
- Certain routines, like preparing meals and grocery shopping, feel manageable, even comforting.
- Being present and available for your family or your job is much more doable. And now you care somewhat about being there whereas before you were just forcing it and faking it.
- You can laugh and enjoy certain moments without instantly feeling the crushing weight of guilt.

Grief is still very much with you but it has loosened its vice grip. You begin to see that life can hold both sorrow and joy.

The 4th G: Growing in Hope

With your momentum in full swing, you have more good days than bad. Hope for a meaningful future is kindled and continues to build. Your emotional resilience is stronger, allowing you to bounce back easier and faster when sorrow temporarily sends you plunging back to feeling Gutted or Grinding. The more hope you allow yourself to feel and nurture, the more progress you make.

Signs of Growing in Hope:

- You make plans and can name things you're genuinely looking forward to doing.
- You take better care of yourself because the future no longer looks bleak… it holds the promise of possibility and opportunity.
- You're able to support others, not just survive yourself.
- You experience joy more often, and you let yourself enjoy those moments a little longer each time.
- You create new habits and methods for maintaining your connection to your loved one.

This period is about realizing you can grow strong within grief. Hope no longer feels like a betrayal. It feels like honoring life, your loved one's and your own.

The 5th G: Grateful

When you're in the Grateful period, you feel a quiet contentment. You focus on the gift of your loved one's life rather than their absence. Gratitude flows in a steady current. Life and work activities feel meaningful again. You're not just going through the motions… you're participating, contributing, enjoying.

There's still a deep sadness you carry and hold inside, and you assume it will always be there. You figure this is as good as it gets. And you're okay with that. Grief Plunges (which you'll learn about later in this chapter) are rare, and when they come, your return is swift, like a dolphin breaking the surface, leaving grief trailing behind.

This period is similar to what Kübler-Ross called Acceptance, and what Kessler later expanded into Finding Meaning.

While you may believe this is the final destination, there's still one more place ahead.

The 6th G: Glorious

When you reach Glorious, you arrive at the peak of healing. You're fully present and fully participating in life. You let go of the pain without letting go of your loved one.

You embrace the future with confidence. You experience renewed passion, joy, purpose, and even peace. Your healing and your story are a gift you're willing to share, because you know others need to hear it.

Feeling Glorious doesn't mean grief is magically gone. It means grief and love now move together like breath, inhale and exhale, each essential to the rhythm of life. Even in your Glorious state, the longing for your loved one remains, because love remains. Grief Plunges still happen, but they're accompanied by tranquility and tenderness. Joy and hope float within and around you.

What's a Grief Plunge?

Many people liken intense moments of grief to waves crashing over you when you least expect it. You're blindsided because you're not standing on the shore; you're walking back to your car, keys in hand, thinking you'd made it through the day. In conjunction with my grief model, I call these moments Grief Plunges.

A Grief Plunge is a sudden immersion in grief. This onset of intense anguish and pain sweeps you from steady ground and plunges you into the icy depths of the ocean, back to the raw pain of Gutted. You're overcome with despair, as if no time has passed at all.

We'll revisit this image throughout the book as it's one of the best ways I've found to describe how grief shows up forcefully and unexpectedly.

Grief Plunges can be accompanied by crying, difficulty breathing, and vivid memories of the most heartbreaking moments of your life. You may also feel physical pain, like aching in your chest, stabbing pain in your gut, or nausea. But here's what's most important: **Grief Plunges are not setbacks. They're an unavoidable part of the healing process.**

Grief Plunges happen in each of the 6 G's in varying degrees of intensity and frequency. In Gutted, your first plunge likely comes after a rare moment of distraction. Then the guilt and horror you feel pulls you right back under.

The good news is, you don't stay under.

Grief diminishes, but love remains... like the tide, returning again and again, with its infinite, soothing presence.

After every plunge, you return to where you were. So, if you were Growing in Hope, and you experience a Grief Plunge, afterwards you return to Growing in Hope. The plunge pulls you under but only temporarily. Then you rise, find your balance, and continue forward in your grief transformation.

Conclusion

As you move through the Grief Transformation Model, Grief Plunges begin to feel more like Grief Floats. You may still be plunged into sadness and pain, but you're not drowning.

You begin to float with the grief rather than fight against it. You become increasingly aware that the pain is temporary and will not overtake you.

Grief diminishes, but love remains… like the tide, returning again and again, with its infinite, soothing presence.

Now that you've seen the overview, the next few chapters go over each of the 6 G's in detail, beginning with Gutted.

FOUR

THE 1ST G: GUTTED

My method for dealing with Gutted grief was to read, write, and think. *I actually tried to think my way through losing my son,* as if my mind could engineer a solution for a behemoth wall of pain. I treated grief like a project, like assembling a piece of furniture from IKEA. I wanted instructions, steps, and a plan to follow. Kind of like this:

Step 1 - Select flowers, funeral clothes, casket, songs, burial plot, etc.

Step 2 - Answer the door and receive visitors and casseroles for 3 days

Step 3 - When visitors stop coming, go to bed and stay there as long as possible, 21 days at least, or until your boss says you must come back to work

Step 4 - Read this list of books

Step 5 -Listen to these podcasts

Step 6 - Write in a journal every day

Step 7 - Create a practice of gratitude

And on and on. Of course, instructions are useless, as you

probably already know from having tried some or all of them. *Why don't they freaking work?* As I discovered, our brain can't help with Gutted emotions, except by getting *out* of the way.

Most grieving people, like myself, learn the hard way when trying to "think themselves healed" that 1) it doesn't work, and 2) it leaves you feeling like there's something wrong with your mind.

In the early weeks and months of grief (and sometimes years depending on your loss), some people say they feel like they're going crazy. This is a common and normal feeling, stemming from the Misbeliefs of Grief discussed in Chapter 2, along with the unrealistic expectations people have of you, and that you may also have of yourself, to 'move on' with your life.

When You Stop Running

One Saturday morning was unbearably hard. With no work to bury myself in, I was missing Jackson so much. And I was upset with my (then) husband, so I got in the car and drove to the cemetery. I sat on my navy blue and forest green plaid blanket and wrote in my journal.

I rarely allowed others to see me when I was feeling Gutted. But I was barely staying afloat in the deep end of grief that day, so I decided to drive to my parents' house. Mom had been called into the office, so Dad was home alone. He did his best to take care of me in her absence. "Do you want a ham sandwich? Or some Cold Duck?" he asked.

I shook my head no and slumped onto the couch. It had tiny lavender and burgundy flowers intertwined with deep green vines. I stared ahead, unseeing, at the white stone fireplace.

Dad hesitated, then sat down beside me, resisting the gravitational pull of his recliner and the clicker. "I'm no good at this," he said. But he put his arm around me, and I tilted my head to rest it against his shoulder.

We sat quietly, and he let me cry. I needed that much more than words, advice, clichés, silver linings… just his strong, sunburned arm to lean on. And to know he was there for me and he loved me, even if he wasn't sure how to express it.

Even now, I can't say exactly why I didn't want other people to see me cry or admit to feeling hopeless. Partly, I wanted to protect people from knowing how devastated I really felt. I didn't want them to worry, and if they knew, they most certainly would worry. But thankfully, that one day at least, I let my dad see my pain and I felt better.

As Tanmeet Sethi writes in *Joy Is My Justice*:

"Facing your pain feels like danger. But it's also a deeply human act to face pain and lovingly know it is yours to transform."

Eventually, I learned that avoiding and hiding your feelings leads to a much longer healing journey. Feelings of pain and anguish must be allowed to flow. This lets the sad energy out and creates space for healing energy to come in.

Vulnerability researcher Brené Brown explained it this way in an interview on *60 Minutes*: "Let me tell you this for sure, and I know this from my life… from 20 years of research, and 400,000 pieces of data. If you don't name what you're feeling, if you don't own the feelings and feel them, they will eat you alive."[5]

In other words, they will remain unhealed wounds that you carry with you indefinitely. The more you push the feelings down, the more you prolong your grief transformation. As often as you're able, let the emotions flow up and out.

If Time Healed, We'd All Be Fine

You know that ridiculous saying, "Time heals all wounds?" It's not true. The mere fact of time passing doesn't heal emotional wounds. Left unexpressed, these painful emotions can cause physical pain in our bodies. As Stephen Levine explains in *Unattended Sorrow*, grief that goes unattended often "manifests in various ways - a weakening of the body, a diminishment of energy, sleep disturbances…"

If the idea of emotional pain impacting your body seems a little too "woo" or over-the-top, ask yourself what was going on in your life when you had physical symptoms like these:

- tension in your shoulders, neck, and back
- a rock in your stomach
- extreme fatigue
- heaviness in your chest
- headaches
- clenched teeth or jaw
- insomnia

Physical symptoms of emotional pain are common in the Gutted period. According to Levine, that's no coincidence, and it points to the mind-body connection. This can even shed light on what may be going on when we feel like our grief is making us crazy.

The other day, after an especially intense CrossFit workout, I was reminded of one of the most disorienting physical symptoms of early grief—brain fog and feeling detached from reality. In my most foggy moments, I would feel highly irritated if someone tried to start a conversation with me. That's because I was barely holding myself together; I couldn't think or talk. I could barely breathe.

If someone did persist in talking to me, they would probably notice my glassy gaze and feel like Chris Tucker trying to talk to Jackie Chan when he first steps off the plane in the movie *Rush Hour;* "Do you speak English? Do you understand the words coming out of my mouth?" The answers would be "yes" and "yes," but I couldn't respond in an appropriate manner. *My brain wasn't functioning.*

When I first learned about the mind-body connection, I was relieved. My insomnia, my neck and shoulders in knots, the rock in my stomach, my chest caved in, drawing my heart inward for protection… these weren't signs of weakness or inability to cope. My body was storing and holding on to the pain *until I could process it.*

As Tanmeet Sethi explains, "What your mind and heart cannot resolve, your body will hold onto." We heal our physical symptoms of grief by releasing emotional pain. Sounds easy enough. *Yeah, right.*

Why Do We Hide And Avoid Our Feelings?

We experience loss events throughout our lives, beginning in childhood. If you ever had to move to a new town or even "just" to a new school as a kid, that was a major transition, a painful experience, a loss to be grieved.

Pretending to be fine may put others at ease, but it cuts us off from support and deepens our sense of isolation.

But no one teaches us to grieve these life changes. Society doesn't encourage us to acknowledge our life-transition losses, much less take time to honor our legitimate feelings like sadness, anxiety, and fear. We're told to be brave. Smile. Move on.

So we learn to hide our tears and feelings and just try to move on from one painful life transition to another continuing into adulthood. According to *The Grief Recovery Handbook,* "Society literally teaches us to *act recovered.*" Pretending to be fine may put others at ease, but it cuts us off from support and deepens our sense of isolation.

When loss hits, whether it's a death or a major life upheaval, our learned response is to ignore our painful feelings, not resolve them.

Grief Companion Corner: Afraid About What Else Could Happen

Dear Jennifer,

After my son died, at first I was in shock. Now reality is sinking in and I'm afraid. I fear for my other son and losing someone else. Every freaking thing about how they might be in danger from just normal living, eating, driving. I can't stop worrying. Am I going crazy?

Yours truly,
—Afraid

Dear Afraid,

You're not going crazy. When the unthinkable happens to you, you start to imagine all kinds of previously unthinkable things might also happen. And just because you're thinking about your son or other loved ones dying and worrying about it, that doesn't mean it's a sign of any kind. You're going through the grief process and being scared and anxious is a part of that process.

A few things that helped me manage my fear and anxiety were talking out loud to my son, writing letters to him, reading books, talking to trusted friends, and focusing on the present moment… just taking one step and one task at a time. Brush your teeth. Get dressed. Eat something. Drink water. Breathe. One thing at a time.

If you feel like your fear is unmanageable, please call a therapist. Sometimes professional help is necessary.

Love and hugs,
Jennifer

Dragonflies and Transitional Objects

In the early evening, on day two of planning my son's funeral, the doorbell rang. I opened it to find my four best neighborhood friends whom I hadn't seen since they got the news about Jackson. They rushed inside, and we crumpled to the ground crying on the cold tile in the entryway. I don't remember what was said, but I do remember feeling thankful for their presence. They must have been nervous, unsure of how to act or what to say, but they were brave and showed up anyway. And they brought two special gifts.

The first gift was a story by Doris Hickney called *Waterbugs and Dragonflies.* In a parable of the afterlife, the waterbugs scurry around in the mud and muck of the pond (life on earth), and eventually, they crawl to the surface (the afterlife) and transform into dragonflies. The waterbugs are heartbroken as their loved ones leave the water never to be seen again. *What happened to them?* they wonder. So, the waterbugs make a pact that after they reach the surface, they'll return and let everyone know they're okay.

But once the waterbugs climb the lily stalk and transform into dragonflies, as they try to re-enter the pond, they bounce off the water. There's no way for them to go back. They realize someday their loved ones will become dragonflies, too, and join them. And so they fly off into their beautiful new world of sunshine and air.

After reading the story, I remember saying, "I don't want Jackson to be a dragonfly. I want him to be a waterbug and be here with me!" Still, imagining him enjoying his new life as a dragonfly, soaring the skies in the *beyond,* it was a comforting vision.

After reading the dragonfly story, I opened the second gift. It was a silver necklace with a James Avery dragonfly charm. I wore that necklace every day for at least a year. *It was like a conduit of connection between me and Jackson.* Throughout the day, I'd rub the charm between my thumb and index finger, pressing it against my skin, close to my heart… remembering my beautiful boy and telling him, "I love you. I miss you. Stay close. Help me."

Having a physical object that I could touch and see... it validated that yes, I am still a mom and I do have a son even if he isn't physically here on this earth. I later learned objects like these are considered 'transitional objects' or 'linking objects.' These are physical objects that help you remember your loved one, honor the life they lived, and continue to feel close to them.

Transitional objects can also be useful even when you're not coping with a death. My daughter is in college now, and on the days I find myself missing her more than usual, I take out her childhood teddy bear and hold it close as I fall asleep. It's simple yet surprisingly comforting.

Finding a symbol that makes us feel an ongoing connection to our loved one can be like a life preserver when we're Gutted. In the later G's, your transitional objects may help you recover from the overwhelm of grief faster - to turn Grief Plunges into Hope Floats.

The Shuttle Run of Grief

One day, about a month after Jackson died, one of the girls in my support group suggested writing letters directly *to* Jackson in my journal. *What a great idea.* Pouring my heart out and telling Jackson everything was a tremendous relief. Here's what I wrote to him about three months after he passed. (Warning, it's pretty sad. But sad was how I felt and what I needed to write about).

August 28, 2003

Jackson, I miss you so much. I think today not having you here with me is making me physically ill. I had to leave work and come home and crawl in bed. I haven't done that since you left us almost three months ago.

I've been going to work every day and trying so hard to survive, but I don't know how to keep doing that because it's not making me feel better; it's not *helping me to miss you less or hurt less or want you back less. In fact, I hurt more and want you back more desperately than ever.*

It shouldn't be this way. It's not fair and I don't understand.

I love you so very much sweet boy. Please watch over me.

This letter is a good example of the constant movement, back and forth, between moments of being able to function and moments of collapse. Most days I could press on through work. Other days I was sick in bed. I shifted from Grinding to Gutted and back again.

As much as I tried to illustrate this back-and-forth movement within the 6 G's of Grief Transformation, no model can fully capture the messy, tumultuous reality.

The trouble with ladders, pyramids, hierarchies, or numbered stages is that they suggest a linear journey, like progressing from kindergarten through senior year. They imply you graduate from one phase to the next and never go back.

But grief doesn't cooperate with constructs. **Instead of moving in orderly steps, grief resists forward motion, drags you back, and makes you cover the same ground again and again.**

Moving between the 6 gradations of grief is like a *shuttle run*: messy, exhausting, and full of backtracking. Remember those orange cones in the days of elementary school P.E.? You start at Cone 1. Then you sprint to Cone 2 and back to Cone 1. Then to Cone 3, and back to Cone 1. Then Cone 4… and back again. This is the shuttle run of grief, only far less orderly than the foot-tangling exercise you may remember from childhood.

You begin your shuttle run at Gutted. Initially, you may be in shock and feel numb, and after that you feel the unbearable weight of loss. You're devastated. You're living in the aftermath of horrifying tragedy. This is Gutted.

At times you'll take a Grinding step forward. You get out of bed, rinse the dirty dishes and load them into the dishwasher. Then you notice their maroon mug, the one that says "I'm not for everyone" sitting on the dish towel. This sends you back to bed, back to Gutted.

You likely move between Gutted and Grinding continuously for months. You may venture out and feel something like Gaining Momentum on occasion, and then you'll resume alternating between Gutted and Grinding once again.

This shuttle run continues for months and years, and your timeline will be unique to you.

As you shuttle along, you'll find that eventually, your home base changes. You'll spend an increasing amount of time able to accomplish daily tasks, with a huge amount of grinding effort. But still, you're somewhat functioning, and that's when your home base changes from Gutted to Grinding. That's progress!

But even after your home base changes, you'll still return to Gutted. This is the shuttle run of grief… forward and back, forward and back, slowly healing as you go.

Conclusion

The Gutted period feels like a series of endless shuttle runs. There's no defined timeline or transition from one period to another, but one thing is certain: the road is long.

You can't sprint through grief. It's not a 5K, or even a 500K, with a finish line and a red ribbon to break through. You can try, like I did, to work your way through it, think your way through it, or avoid it, but you can't escape the shuttle runs of grief.

So, what do you do during the endless days of the in-between?

You take tiny steps. And remind yourself:

- The pain will be intense, but it will not overtake you.
- Even when it doesn't seem possible, you will survive.
- You can honor your pain in small, manageable doses.
- Treat yourself tenderly as you learn, day by day, to live without your loved one.

Love that is lost hurts.
Pain calls for your presence.
Feeling opens the door to healing.

You can't sprint through grief. It's not a 5K, or even a 500K, with a finish line and a red ribbon to break through.

You may not be able to see it yet, but every hard-won lap of the shuttle run carries you closer to a new home base. This brings us to the next G – Grinding.

FIVE

THE 2ND G: GRINDING

Your Gutted and Grinding periods might look very different than mine. However you get through Grinding, you're just putting one foot in front of the other and teaching yourself to live without your loved one in the world. This can feel like re-learning how to walk after being in a coma.

You may feel depressed and angry, which may cause you to retreat from others and try to be self-reliant at a time when the biggest benefit would come from leaning on others to find your balance.

I spent a lot of time Grinding. As I've mentioned, I'm stubbornly independent and quite adept at compartmentalizing my feelings. I returned to work three days after the funeral, and I functioned. The effort was Grinding, but I suspect most people had no idea because I was trying to be strong.

People must have thought I was truly crazy at Jackson's visitation. I sat and chatted like it was a birthday party or a family reunion. I particularly remember sitting on the couch with my friend, Cindy, who I hadn't seen since leaving my corporate job six years prior. "Thank you for coming," I said. "Tell me how you're doing."

She said, "You don't want to hear about my little life. *Do you?*"

"Yes, I really do," I said. "I have the rest of my life to mourn and grieve. Right now, a distraction is good. So, tell me what you've been up to."

During the luncheon after the funeral, I visited with everyone and laughed at their stories. I imagine they thought I'd downed a few shots outside or swallowed a couple Xanax. But I was doing my habitual thing—put the feelings in a box, shut the lid, and focus on something else.

There were few times I ever asked anyone for help. Years later, I finally began to understand why asking for help felt nearly impossible. My coach Diana posed a question that caught me off guard:

"Jennifer," she asked, "Did anyone ever teach you how to ask for help growing up?"

I distinctly recall my answer, "No! They didn't teach me how to *ask* for help. They taught me not to *need* help, ever."

The realization landed hard. My parents weren't uncaring; far from it. They were devoted and loving. But independence was a necessity in our home. My parents both worked full-time jobs so we kids had to take care of ourselves from a young age. If we were sick, we still went to school (and as we got older, to work). If we were sad, we had ten minutes to feel it. Then it was time to pull ourselves together.

They taught us about perseverance and doing what had to be done. They could never have imagined how far I would take that lesson. Not only did I internalize the value of independence, I took it to an extreme.

And I unconsciously armored myself against vulnerability, and I developed a deep resistance to receiving care. That fierce independence, paired with my discomfort around being vulnerable, shaped how I moved through the world in grief. I didn't slow down. I pressed on and pushed harder.

Running on Sheer Will

Throughout the early months and years after Jackson died, I was incredibly restless. I couldn't sleep, couldn't sit still or enjoy TV like

I did before... *who cares about American Idol when your baby is dead?* So, I stayed monumentally busy, which was pretty much necessary after having two more kids, getting divorced, and working a full-time, demanding job.

I remember many times I was up all night feeling overwhelmed with life and grief, and in the morning I'd wake up thinking, *I don't think I can do this.* Thankfully, there was another part of me that said, *I'm going to try. I'm going to get up and try.* Most of the time I managed to get dressed and get to work. And even managed to get some work done. Massive accomplishment! But every day wasn't like that.

One really hard morning, the "I don't think I can do this" scenario played out. I forced myself out of bed, showered, got dressed, packed lunch, and left the house. I parked my Tahoe in my unofficial parking spot up front and just sat there... trying to pump myself up to get out of the car and through the front door.

I was crying, trying to pull myself together. As I shook my head, debating as to whether I could in fact '*do this,*' a vehicle pulled up beside me.

The driver lowered his window and waved to get my attention. I snapped out of my inner struggle and pushed the button to lower my window. There was Wally, one of the foremen, looking very surprised and concerned. He had red hair, round ruddy cheeks, and soft blue eyes. He said, "I noticed your lights were on. Just wanted to make sure you turned them off..."

I turned the knob for the lights and said, "Oh, okay. Thanks."

I don't recall if anything else was said, but a question he didn't ask lingered in the air... *Are you okay? Are you going to be okay?* And kindness lingered, too, *I'm so sorry. I didn't know it was still this bad. I wish there was something I could do.*

I didn't make it into the office that day. Most days, though, I pushed through the fog. I got up, showed up, and kept moving. And in hindsight, I think the structure helped more than I realized.

People made fun of me for how rigidly I stuck to the schedule, but that's how I controlled things and held myself and our family together.

For many years, I devoted all my energy into creating a safe bubble for myself and my two subsequent children. Mostly, we stayed at home as a family unit and rarely made plans with others. I had walls up between me and everyone except my kids. People made fun of me for how rigidly I stuck to the schedule, but that's how I controlled things and held myself and our family together. The only opposite of our routine that I could imagine was the chaos of Gutted and out of control. *No, thank you.*

Tiny Connections Can Carry Us

The move toward letting people in can start small. The mental health community widely acknowledges the importance of tiny interactions between strangers, dubbed 'weak ties.' However, I think of them more like 'minor ties' because although these relationships may not be our deepest connections, they aren't necessarily *weak*.

Litsa Williams, author, therapist, and co-founder of *What's Your Grief,* notes that we're often "looking to a barista for an emotional boost."[6]

Brief social exchanges with salesclerks and restaurant servers become even more significant in grief, when we feel disconnected from ourselves and withdrawn from others.

While Grinding can leave us feeling remote from loved ones and friends, minor ties allow us to feel human again, however briefly, and give us a dose of togetherness. The conversation is mutually low-risk, high-reward because your grocery clerk doesn't expect you to tell them your innermost feelings, and we don't expect them to listen, anyway. Yet, the lightness and friendliness of a brief encounter can lift the cloud of grief, at least a little.

Williams writes that these small connections provide a "buffer against stress and loneliness and [are] linked to improved cognitive function and reduced mortality risk." [6] The next time an Uber driver or grocery store clerk is chatty, lean in.

Gifts of Help

A couple years ago, I read Jennie Allen's book, *Find Your People*, which reminded me how isolated I allowed myself to become as I Grinded on. I recognized myself in Jennie's description of her own tendency and that of Western society: "We don't come together in our pain. We isolate. We insulate. We pretend. We call *after* the cry."

Yep, this is me to a "T"… except I don't even call after the cry. Thankfully, my people found *me* and didn't say "Call me if you need anything." They just took action.

My sister-in-law spent the night one of the first nights after Jackson died. I had to get up at 2:30am to pump because my breasts were full, and I had no baby to feed. I was sitting on the living room floor behind the couch where I could plug in the pump. Robin crept in, sat on the floor next to me, and asked if I was in pain. I said, "Yes" and began crying. She hugged me and comforted me. I don't remember words… just that she was there in one of the most unbelievably painful moments of my life.

My little sister, Brenda, came to stay in the guest room for several months immediately following Jackson's death. She dropped her summer classes and moved to town to be with me and, OMG, what an amazing gift. I never would have asked her to do that. She just did it, probably knowing that if she'd asked, I would have said, "No, I'm okay."

I'm *so* grateful she made that huge sacrifice to be near, to help, and to see with her own eyes how I was doing. I suspect she also reported back to Kay and the rest of the family who were very concerned and had no idea if I was alright because I wasn't forthcoming with that information.

I knew they wanted me to feel better, and I wanted me to feel better. So I tried, by sheer force of will, to make it happen. You can guess how that worked out.

My friend, Schawn, organized a wonderful tribute to Jackson the Valentine's Day after his passing. She gathered friends, family, and her students to help make Valentine kits for children in local hospitals and Ronald McDonald House. Each kit contained supplies the children could use to create their own Valentine's Day cards. The kits also included a Valentine for the child signed, *"Love, from Jackson."*

In her letter asking for support, she wrote that after Jackson died she didn't know what to do to help. She questioned, "What words or casserole could make any difference?" She said she tried to distract me, entertain me, and help me to forget my pain.

Then one night, God turned a lightbulb on for Schawn:

"Jennifer doesn't want to forget Jackson and she doesn't want me to either. He was a gift from God, proof of His grace and love, and here I was trying to put the memory of him away."

She closed her letter saying the Valentine's kit project "gives joy to a child at a time in their life when it's hard to come by. And it also serves to let Jennifer know her child is remembered and his life made a difference to us, and in turn, every child we serve through this project." What a tremendous friend and beautiful gesture I'll never forget.

Another huge amount of support came from dear friends, Ken and Corinne. They showed up for me in the most wonderful and unexpected ways, and they never stopped. They surprised me one Saturday morning, arriving at a 5K charity run, each of their family members wearing t-shirts with Jackson's picture. They remembered Jackson's birth and death dates every year. They visited his grave and left mementos for me to find… toys, shells, rocks, flowers, Easter bunnies, pumpkins, tiny Christmas trees, snow globes. To this day, I still find flowers and items they leave at the cemetery, so I know my sweet boy hasn't been forgotten.

I'm able to move through my resistance to accepting help (and admitting I need help) a *little* easier now, having learned from Jennie Allen:

> ➤ We aren't meant to do life alone, hiding behind our beautifully decorated *closed* doors.
> ➤ I must stop trying to *handle everything* by myself.
> ➤ I need to find my people and let them be there for me.

If you're Grinding, look around and try inviting people in. Ask them to call or text to check in, to pray for you, or drop off a meal. People want to help. When you give them a few simple suggestions, you make it easier on them, and you.

Grief Companion Corner: Wondering About God

Dear Jennifer,

I've always believed in a higher power, and when my grandson was born with complications, I prayed like never before. He had the most beautiful smile, but he died at age five months. I've always had faith, but right now my relationship with God is on hold.

Yours truly,
—Shaky Faith

Dear Shaky Faith,

Many people question God and their faith when faced with a tragic loss so first off, know that you're not alone in feeling this way. Perhaps this Chinese parable will be of some comfort.

A woman lost her son, and she went to the elder of the community and asked him to save her from the terrible pain. He told her to go to a house that had never known sorrow and bring back some mustard seeds from that home. They would use the seeds to drive the pain out of her heart. So she set off to find a home that had never known sorrow.

She came upon a huge mansion and thought, "Surely these people who have such great wealth and luxury have never known sorrow. I will get my mustard seeds here." She knocked on the door and told the mistress of the home her story. The lady told her she would have to look elsewhere because her home did know sorrow, and in fact her husband lay dying upstairs, suffering from a painful disease.

The woman thought she could help this family, having endured a loss of her own, so went in and ministered to the husband and his wife. After a few days, she set off on her search again. In one home after another, the woman found a tale of sorrow and continued to minister to the families. And in doing so, little by little, she began to feel better.

After her lengthy search, she finally went back to the elder and told him there were no homes that had never known sorrow but that she didn't need the mustard seeds anymore because in giving to others, her heart had healed.

You said your relationship with God is on hold which is totally understandable. And He can handle it while you work through your grief. In the meantime, perhaps this parable adds some perspective. We're not alone in our suffering, and a tremendous amount of healing can come from helping others.

Love and hugs,
Jennifer

The Question of God

Although I was stubborn and made the Grinding period harder on myself by trying to be strong and hiding my pain, all the big and small offers of connection and support were nudging me into Gaining Momentum. But first there was another relationship I had to mend… my relationship with God.

As I said to Shaky Faith, many people experience a crisis of faith when a life-shattering blow hits. The unrelenting questions of "Why? Why me? Why my family? Why did God let this happen?" can haunt you day and night. I tackled these questions as I did everything else… by reading and learning what others had gone through and how they survived.

What I discovered was so helpful to me that I wrote a short ebook summarizing my key takeaways. It's called *How to Shut Down the Unrelenting Question, "WHY, God?"* (see Resources section for a link).

Of course, answers to questions don't bring your loved one back, but they can help you move beyond endlessly asking, "Why did this happen?" and, instead, begin wondering, "What will I do now?"

Even though I asked "Why?" repeatedly, for months and years, I never blamed God or felt He persecuted me intentionally. But I did stop going to church for a long while.

The few times I tried attending service after Jackson's death, I was a wreck. I cried inconsolably, shoulders bobbing with each gasping breath and my nose running profusely. That was *uncomfortable* for me and the poor strangers nearby who presumably wondered, *Is that lady going to be alright?*

When I finally returned to a church home, the pastor was preaching a series called "Baggage" and he shared a story about a family ski trip. His sons hauled their overstuffed suitcases across the terminal. Pastor Randy watched them struggle, lugging and adjusting the bags several times until his youngest son stopped and asked, "Dad, will you carry these for me?"

The point, of course, is that God is there too, waiting for us to come to Him with our stuff and say, "Dad, can you carry this?" He wants us to give Him our "baggage." He'll gladly carry it. And I knew this to be true because I'd prayed for help and comfort, and I received it.

God doesn't hurt us with undeserved pain, but He does help us with undeserved blessings.

When we're Grinding, we're like the pastor's sons slogging through life with our heavy load. I remember wondering though, *"Am I supposed to ask God to free me from the pain?"*

The pain persisted because of the love. And I didn't want that to disappear. Thus I resisted letting go of my "baggage." I wanted to keep hauling it around with me. I wasn't ready to let it go. I was *afraid* to let it go.

I couldn't imagine a day when I would pack up my pain, hand it over to God, and let Him carry it away. But I tried to be open to the possibility.

What nudged me forward was the pastor's key point: unhealed wounds (baggage) hurt your relationships... with others and with God. And they keep you from your full potential and purpose.

As I tried to find my way to purpose, this truth became my anchor: *God doesn't hurt us with undeserved pain, but He does help us with undeserved blessings.*

What If I Can't?

Holding on to God and the promise of purpose gave me strength. And I managed to carry my grief and keep going. But I met so many people who had a different experience... who needed support and couldn't find it.

That's why I created a service to send encouraging texts to grievers in the early days of grief.

One day, while crafting a message, I came across this simple yet brilliant quote from Michele Deville: "When you can—you will."[7]

I shared Deville's quote with my support group along with these words:

Heartbreaking loss disrupts everything in your life. And what used to be an ordinary activity suddenly feels like an insurmountable feat.

Whenever a thing feels insurmountable, know that it's okay if you just don't do it.

It's okay if you don't:

➢ go to the party
➢ take a shower
➢ cook dinner
➢ respond to calls/texts

And also know, there's no timeframe after which you're no longer allowed to give yourself grace. It may be four months after your loss or four years. The hard days and seemingly insurmountable things will come along.

Be patient with yourself knowing: when you can, you will.

———

I could've really used this advice in my early days of grief. I remember feeling so afraid that if I let myself fully feel the depth of my pain, I'd crawl into bed and never come out.

Thankfully, Deville's words turned out to be true. I did what I could, when I could. I didn't stay in bed and cry forever.

Which reminds me of a conversation I had with my son many years later.

Conclusion

One night, Jake asked me what I would do if he died. I told him I would cry, SO much, and never stop. He was skeptical. "But Jackson died, and you don't cry anymore," he said.

I replied, "Actually, I do. I still miss him. And sometimes I cry."

"Really? When? I don't see you…"

He wasn't sure what to believe because I don't cry often. And when I do, it's in the shower. In the car. Or my closet. Out of sight.

Grief doesn't disappear like people think it does. It just becomes more private. More invisible.

And that's one of the hardest parts about Grinding through grief: *You're carrying what no one else sees and trying to function in a world that assumes you're fine.*

And yet, slowly, things do begin to shift.

One afternoon, about eight months after Jackson's death, I experienced a change. I walked by his door after work, and for the first time, I didn't duck inside to sit in the rocker and cry. I kept walking. And I felt a flicker of something I hadn't felt in ages… a glimmer of hope that life could be more than sleepless nights and going through the motions by day.

I was finally Gaining Momentum.

Six

The 3rd G:
Gaining Momentum

When the home base of your grief shuttle run changes from Grinding to Gaining Momentum, you may not be aware because the shift is incremental, almost imperceptible.

C.S. Lewis says of this gradual change, there's "no sudden, striking, and emotional transition. Like the warming of a room or the coming of daylight. When you first notice them they have already been going on for some time."

Each action creates motion that increases your energy, so you're not constantly depleted.

As I waited for time to heal my aching heart, every morning, I put on my survival armor, went to work, talked to clients, created spreadsheets and financial reports. Through it all, I held back the tears, saving them until I got back home for "crying time."

This journal entry outlines the torrent of feelings I had no idea how to manage.

September 28, 2003

Dear Jackson,

I don't know how I'm supposed to live without you. It's just so hard. I miss you terribly, and I always will. I don't want to do this. I don't want to see other babies and wish they were you.

I don't want to be jealous of other people when I see them and their babies everywhere I go — the grocery store and Starbucks and all over the neighborhood and restaurants and even work when Sarah brings Kiley. That's not fair.

Why do they have their babies, and I don't have you? I don't understand, and it's hard to accept that I never will. I want to go back in time. I want to have another three months with you. No, I want to have the three months and a lifetime with you. I don't want to go to the cemetery to visit you. I hate this.

Sometimes I can focus on the absolute joy of the time I did have with you. I'll try to get in that frame of mind again, sweetie. I know you don't want me to be sad or angry. I know you're happy where you are. Help me, Jackson. Help me to find some peace.

I love you to the moon.

That final paragraph signals an effort to shift in my grief. I was focusing on feelings and ideas that enabled me to commune with my son's memory and his soul without feeling Gutted or barely able to Grind out one more day.

In *A Heart That Works*, Rob Delaney reflects on the life of his son, Henry. He writes, "In between Henry's birth and his death was, of course, his life. That was my favorite part."

That was my favorite part too, Jackson's life. In focusing on the gift of his presence, rather than the pain of his absence, I was transforming my feelings of loss and moving toward the joy and gratitude Delaney describes.

This chapter focuses on practical things you can do to increase healing momentum: Chasing Shade, Turn Down the Dial, Block People Who Aren't Helping You, Shift Focus and Find Balance with 80/20, and Live Like They're Not Gone.

The key is to add more habits and people who pull you toward healing and reduce obstacles in the way of your progress. Repeating your positive habits over and over can even swing you to the next G, Growing in Hope.

Chasing Shade

When I get hot, I don't sweat like a normal person. My feet and my head sweat a smidge, but the rest of me doesn't. Consequently, I get overheated and suffer from heat exhaustion easily and often. So I have to be creative to survive my daily CrossFit workouts.

The worst are when the workouts involve running... outside in sunny, unbearably hot San Antonio, Texas. I wear a cold towel around my neck and carry a spray bottle of ice cold water to spritz on my ears. I even pour it all over my head when the thermometer is upwards of 105 degrees.

On these runs, I feel like Count Drac in the movie *Transylvania*, running through town in the daylight, zigging and zagging to avoid the crisping sun, finding a patch of relief when the townspeople form a human tunnel for him. Similarly, I run from one patch of shade, into the sun, my skin singeing, until I find the next patch of shade.

The only way to manage the scorching heat is to set tiny goals... make it to the four-way-stop. If I can go a little farther, continue to the mailbox stand. If not, rest there, breathe, then start again. Next target: porch with rocking chairs. Then the basketball hoop. After that, black Chevy Silverado. Then the boulder by the crosswalk. Maybe even catch up to Gyllian. Each landmark, a finish line and a starting line, a way to keep moving when the whole thing feels like a blistering nightmare.

One day while running I realized this is exactly how it is with grief... you have to find a way to bear the unbearable. The only way I found was to break it down into tiny pieces. Survive this hour. Make it through this day. Rest when I can't go anymore. Then pick a new target and start again.

Here's what you need to know: You can create your own shade, one patch at a time. Start with small self-care activities like naps, warm baths to loosen tense muscles, stepping outside for fresh air, stretching, or sipping a cup of coffee. You might sleep holding a teddy bear or other stuffed animal. Joining a support group or talking to a therapist are also great ways to find relief.

If you've tried these things and felt like they didn't work, remember Gaining Momentum isn't about doing something once. You create emotional shade by turning your momentum activities into habits and routines. The more of these activities you do regularly, the more shade you create.

Later in your healing journey, you may lean into new practices like reading books that teach you how to live with grief while also choosing life, journaling with prompts that move you toward deeper healing, music that lifts your spirit, or acts of kindness that bring light to others.

You create emotional shade by turning your momentum activities into habits and routines.

Shade even comes in the form of people. You may widen your support network to include friends who can listen. That's what happened to me when a stranger offered me the gift of being seen and heard.

A Brave Soul Who Leaned In

One weekday morning, I stopped at my neighborhood Starbucks. I sat by the window in my favorite chair, the comfy beige one with flat arms, wide enough to hold my coffee and my book.

Watching the morning commuters come in for their daily lattes, caramel macchiatos, and green teas, I thought how I used to be like them… focused on the day ahead and clueless that disaster could strike at any moment.

I took a sip from my cup and picked up my book, *Healing After Loss* by Martha Hickman, trying to concentrate on her meditation for the day.

A pretty blond girl sat quietly in the comfy chair across from me. I glanced up briefly, then returned to my book. A few minutes passed. Then she leaned over, and in a soft voice said, "Can I interrupt you for a minute?"

I looked up again, ready to say, "No, thanks," expecting her to mention Pampered Chef or Mary Kay.

She continued, "This is going to sound so crazy. I've seen you here a few times. The barista is a friend, and I asked him about you. He told me about your son. I hope that's alright."

I blinked and waited for her to continue, wondering where this was headed.

"I just see the pain in your eyes and all around you, and I had to say something. I'm Stacy. I know my story's not the same, but I miscarried twins. It was a long time ago, and I'm fine now, but I just felt I had to talk to you…" she took a sip from her green and white cup. "If you don't want to talk I get it. That's all. I'll stop now. Just please know you can talk to me anytime."

I don't know if I took her up on the offer that very day or if I waited until the next visit. But I accepted. What a kind and beautiful offer it was. To step into my mess and offer to listen? Knowing there would be tears and awkward moments. *Mind boggling.* Most people took one look at me and ran away, fast. She offered me a lifeline that shifted me from Grinding to Gaining Momentum.

Stacy and I met for coffee most weekday mornings from then on. She's a rare human who can discuss complex emotions, painful and tragic life circumstances, and share keen insight. Although she intended to be a shoulder I could lean on, she wound up leaning on me, too. Which made our relationship all the better. We would talk for hours. Sometimes I didn't make it to the office until late morning, something I never would have allowed before the earth was pulled out from under me and I fell into Gutted/Grinding oblivion.

We often laugh about when she first approached me, she thought she would be my champion, and then I became hers, too. I don't know how I would've survived without those talks; they were one of a cluster of new habits I was forming that helped me tell my story, process my pain, and be more present with myself and others.

Our daily coffee conversations became one of my most important patches of shade… a place where I could rest from the burning pain of grief. Every life-affirming action brings you from avoiding your feelings to being present with them, which increases your shade.

Grief Companion Corner: Fear of Crying

Dear Jennifer,

Why am I having such a hard time when I've been a widow for two years? I should want to go into my husband's woodworking shed and be with all his things. I think I want to, I'm just afraid of crying. It's almost like, if I cry, that will be a major setback. I've been doing so well lately, and crying will send me back to Day One.

Thank you for listening.
—Afraid of Crying

Dear Afraid of Crying,

I think you're very right about why you feel so afraid to go into the shed. You're afraid of crying and going backward instead of forward. I've avoided many situations for fear of really losing control. Going into Jackson's room has not been one of those things, but everyone is different.

Recently there was a candlelight memorial service here in my town, and I wanted to go. But I knew it would be emotionally exhausting, and I wasn't ready to put myself through that.

A few days after the memorial service, I had myself a very long cry. And I felt better. I was reluctant to go back to the raw grief, but I had to. Because the pressure kept building inside me, and I had to let it release.

You need to cry. It will happen when it's time to happen. Crying doesn't mean you haven't made progress in your journey. We slowly heal by going up and down, forward and back, and that's just the way grief works. Don't force yourself to go into the shed if you really don't feel up to it. One day, you'll be ready. You'll probably have a good long cry, and I think you'll feel better afterward.

Love and hugs,
Jennifer

Turn Down The Dial

When we're Gutted, strong emotions and spinning thoughts feel uncontrollable, striking like startling claps of thunder in a midnight storm. Then in Grinding, we create mental static, filling every minute with distractions and tasks, to avoid landing on the frequency where we'll hear the noise of our sadness.

But, what if we can manage our thoughts and grief like turning down the volume dial on a radio? John Acuff suggests this in his book, *Soundtracks*. Of course, turning down the volume on grief isn't as easy as flipping a switch one time. It is, however, a learned skill you can practice, and with repetition, it becomes easier.

In the beginning of our grief journey, we need to turn down the dial because we must have a break from the enormous grief and pain that is constant level 10. We can't live in that space for indefinite periods of time.

Later on, when you don't feel continuous grief, you may still need "turn down the dial" techniques to balance grief with daily life as well as Grief Plunges. These activities can help you Gain Momentum and turn the dial back to the emotional state you were in before grief escalated to the level of overwhelm.

Here are some of the go-to actions I take to turn the emotional volume down. I hope you'll try some of these strategies and also add activities to create a list that works for you.

Turn-Down-The-Dial Activities

Physical Activities

- Strength Training: CrossFit is my daily escape. I love the satisfaction of pushing myself and getting stronger. But you might also run, play tennis or pickle-ball, dance, or bike. Exercise is a win-win. You improve your physical health and also improve your emotional health at the same time.
- Yoga: Hatha is a gentle type of yoga as well as Grief Yoga® (created by Paul Denniston). Pilates, Tai-Chi, and stretching are great ways to find tranquility.
- Leaving the house: Take a walk through a grocery store, shopping mall, or office building. Even going for a drive works. The change of scenery will create an opportunity to clear your mind and reset.

Calming Activities

- Coloring: I'm not a "creative" person. I don't make wreaths or gift baskets or do stenciled wall art. But coloring is a simple creative act that doesn't require you to exert energy or think. It's a practice that lets your body and brain rest. To make it even more healing, choose pictures that remind you of your loved one.

- Petting my dog: The rhythmic motion is calming and studies show interacting with pets releases endorphins. If you don't have a pet, wrap yourself up in a soft, cozy blanket.

- Listening to music: Maybe Classical music or Indian Flute music. Whatever music gives you energy, peace, and comfort. Turn up music that lifts your spirit to turn the volume down on grief.

- Getting outside: Sit on your front porch, visit a park, go for a walk and breathe fresh air. As a bonus, the sun increases your vitamin D intake.

Connection Activities

- Journaling: Writing is a safe place to put down what you're carrying. Write down your thoughts, feelings, fears, and memories. Or, write notes TO your loved one. Each word on the page is a small release, a way to ease the weight from your heart. (See the Resources section for journal prompts.)

- Random acts of kindness: These uplift my spirits more than most other methods of mood-management. My acts range from smiling at people, complimenting hairstyles and outfits, leaving big tips for servers, buying coffee/food for the car in line behind me, to donating money to people who have a financial need.

Helping people, for me, is one of the most effective ways to turn down the dial on grief, improve my mood, and feel I'm making a difference in the world while also honoring Jackson's life.

Block People Who Aren't Helping You

When you're grieving, you need every bit of healing energy you can get. But some people block your healing, standing in your way when you need relief most.

Today, after an intense workout involving two of my most difficult and despised movements (running and barbell front squats), I was lying in front of the fan trying to breathe. My Asics were off. Socks, off. Tank top… still on due to my advanced age, but pulled up to bra level to get *more* air. I noticed my tennis shoe was blocking the airflow to one foot. I kicked it out of the way thinking, *Get away! I need every inch of this air.*

Later I laughed at how strongly I reacted, but it reminded me that when we're grieving, the smallest things can be hugely irritating, triggering, even angering. Especially people who make you feel bad because you're still sad. Or people who are surprised and judgy if you seem to be doing well. They ask, "How can you be going out with friends and having fun? So-and-so has been dead for less than a year." For all they know, they might have witnessed your first moments of happiness in said year and then judged you for it. *Grrrrrrrrr.*

I encourage you to kick these people away just like I did my shoe. Well, don't *actually* kick them, but eliminate them from your life, at least for a time. They don't understand. And you don't need people around who make you feel bad about something beyond their ability to grasp.

You don't owe anyone an explanation for how you're grieving or why you can't spend time with unsupportive, unhelpful people.

Avoid people who decide you've grieved long enough and you

need to get over it now. Also avoid people who make you feel guilty if they see you on a "good day" and judge you for it.

It's up to you to protect your emotional well-being. You don't owe anyone an explanation for how you're grieving or why you can't spend time with unsupportive, unhelpful people.

Shift Focus and Find Balance with 80/20

One of the most powerful tools for gaining momentum in my grief came from my mom's 80/20 rule: spend 80% of your time focused on the good things in life and only 20% focused on the hard things. This simple framework has helped me get out of bed and face the world even on my hardest days.

While it's a great and helpful rule, I didn't always feel so keen about it.

Growing up, my siblings and I were subjected to mom's horrible, downright evil, treatment. She made us smile when we were sad! She'd say, "You've had ten minutes to cry and pout. Now, smile." If we tried to get away with a slight, upturned corner of a lip, she'd say, "Nope, smile like you mean it. I want to see teeth." *SO evil, right?*

Looking back, I realize she taught us a powerful lesson: dwelling on negative things only makes you feel worse. Focusing on positive things makes you feel better. And if the ratio is backwards, and you spend 80% of the time focusing on the challenges and difficult situations in life, you can become miserable over the smaller issues.

Of course, applying the 80/20 rule in grief looks different. *It doesn't mean pretending to be 'happy' or even 'okay' after loss.* In the beginning, the ratio will be 0% Good / 100% Grief. Gradually it can change… 1/99, 5/95, and so on. You can build your emotional tolerance and resilience little by little and slowly move toward flipping the ratio.

One way to limit your time actively grieving is to structure your daily routine and devote the majority of your energy to the essentials… working, caring for kids, running errands, grocery shopping, breathing exercises… whatever you can manage.

Then give grief a place on your calendar, its own time slot. Let's say you set aside 4:00-5:00p.m. for 'crying time.' If a trigger threatens to set you off before then, tell yourself, *No, I'm not going there right now. I'll wait for my crying time.* This strategy may not always work, but it's a good tool to help you function better day to day.

In her book *Healing After Loss,* Hickman wrestles with taking charge of her grief. In her March 6th meditation, she says: "I will revel in the times I can be happy—which is what my loved one would want for me." A couple weeks later in her March 30th meditation, she adds: "To some extent it is in my power to decide when I will let grief take over."

Living by the 80/20 rule in grief isn't about ignoring pain. It's about choosing a healthy balance… acknowledging sadness while also making space for joy, beauty, and what's still good.

Live Like They're Not Gone

As I Gained Momentum, the way I carried Jackson in my heart continued to shift. My love for him was still there… strong as ever. But thinking about him was now tinged with cautious optimism that I could find purpose in my life, if not with him, then in his honor. You can see the difference in this letter I wrote to him when he would've been thirteen months old:

April 3, 2004

Dear Jackson,

The other day on the way home from work I saw a family taking pictures in the bluebonnets. The dad had his son up on his shoulders, and the mom was taking their picture. I felt so sad. That should be us. I should've been taking that picture of you and your dad.

Living without you is so hard, and it seems like it will always be hard. I can't imagine a time when I won't ache for you. Every day for the rest of my life, you will be missing, and I will miss you. Sometimes I don't know what to do with that reality. What I want to do is just go to bed and never get up. To face a lifetime without you is too hard. I should NOT have to do that. I don't know. I don't know what I'm trying to get at. I guess there's no way to explain this kind of grief.

Stacy and I have talked many times about how the loss of a child has so many layers. There's the physical loss first and foremost of course. But there's also so many additional losses:

Your dreams and hopes for the future, the physical act of being a parent, all the everyday things you no longer get to do with your child, the loss of feeling you have some control over what happens in your life, the loss of the naïve bliss of actually believing horrific tragedies only happen to other people, the loss of your old self, the one who died when your child died, and the loss of optimism and hope and faith. The list just goes on and on.

How is it possible to learn to live with so much pain and loss?

Many people never figure out a way. They continue to live physically, but emotionally and spiritually they die. And then there's another whole series of losses for them and their families.

I know you don't want that for us sweet boy. And that's one of the things that keeps me going. I know you're watching over us. And you want us to be happy.

Another thing that keeps me going is that I always planned to be a good mommy and set a good example for you. Well, even though you're not here, I still want to be a good mom, setting a good example *and doing the right thing. It's different now, because you're not learning from me like you would be if you had lived. But I'm still your mom. I'll always be your mom. And I want to keep doing the things a good mom would do. For me that's doing whatever I can to heal, regain my faith and hope, and make you proud of me.*

I love you so much, all the way to the moon, and back.

Conclusion

Every day you can make choices to feel better more often.

Small choices like chasing shade, turning down the dial, and protecting your heart from unhelpful people… they add up and eventually become automatic habits.

This creates increased momentum that helps you carry your loved one with you as you step forward into the next G – Growing in Hope.

SEVEN

THE 4TH G: GROWING IN HOPE

One night while writing, a troubling thought hit me: *What if readers find the "Gutted to Glorious" theme off-putting? I think most would easily understand "Gutted" but "Glorious" might seem like a highly unrealistic, or even unattainable goal.*

Grief Transformation is the "road less traveled." You get to decide to travel the road that leads to 'good enough' or travel the road that leads to 'Glorious.'

I'd wondered about this before and brushed it off, but this time I noticed an idea beneath the surface.

The way I see life and grief reminds me of Robert Frost's famous poem, "The Road Not Taken." The last three lines say:

Two roads diverged in a wood, and I—

I took the one less traveled by,

And that has made all the difference.

Grief Transformation is a road you can choose to travel. It may seem daunting… narrow, uneven, littered with holes and rocks just waiting to trip you. But with effort you navigate the obstacles and arrive to feeling lighter, relieved the road ahead is smoother. You may pause or stop anywhere you like on this path. You get to decide to travel the road that leads to 'good enough' or travel the road that leads to 'Glorious.'

Growing in Hope is one of those forks in the road of grief. This 4th G is the midpoint where you evolve from Gaining Momentum to Growing in Hope. Many people live their entire lives shuttling back and forth between the first three periods, Gutted and barely functioning/non-functioning, Grinding and getting by but with a maximum amount of effort, and Gaining Momentum where they experience moments of relief more often.

Stepping into the second half of transformation and Growing in Hope requires a leap of faith… in yourself, a higher power, and in your loved one.

When you first notice hope blossoming again, you may realize you've had more good days than bad in one or more weeks. When you're reminded of your loved one and losing them, you're bouncing back from sadness more quickly, focusing on the good memories and the love you still carry and hold dear.

As you make this transition, ask yourself, *"What would it mean for me to take the road less traveled and give hope room to grow?"*

For me, it meant choosing:

- To focus more on the gift of having Jackson rather than focus on the pain of losing him.
- To function as much as possible every day, going to work and taking care of my family.
- To read and learn, to gather strength and hope from those who had traveled this road before me.
- To live and set an example for my child, even though he was gone.
- To reinvest and risk my heart in my two subsequent children.
- To do my "grief work" instead of wish and wait for time to heal me.

- To help others and listen to others' stories which helped me to heal (though admittedly this was also a subconscious way of avoiding telling my own story and hiding my pain).

In retrospect, most of these choices were good for me and my growth in and through grief. Your list may be mixed, too, and that's to be expected.

A Lifeline of Friendship

As I continued down the road of grief, I rarely paused to think about how I was doing. When I did, the answer was mixed. Most of the time, I believed my wound was healing, slowly, and it wasn't preventing me from living a happy and productive life. But other times, I thought maybe my grief should be more healed than it was.

Thankfully, I had someone who could help me see things more clearly when I felt confused. A huge impact on my ability to Grow in Hope came from a special friendship with Sam, a kindred spirit in my SIDS support group. Her first son, Zachary, died only a few weeks after Jackson died. Sam and I connected quickly, took our friendship outside the support group, and started emailing daily.

Sharing the brutal truth, with someone who completely understood and was going through the *same* thing, was a lifeline I wouldn't have survived without. Plus, Sam was hilarious so we didn't just cry and mourn. We laughed and lifted each other up on the many hard days.

On one such day, in January of 2011, I was in quite a funk. This was typically *her* time of year to need support as that was Zachary's birth month. But Sam and I had the kind of relationship that I didn't hesitate to email her anyway.

Jan 19, 2011 at 9:56 AM:

Me: I think it pretty much sucks to have to ALWAYS and FOREVER miss our boys … it also sucks to have to sound and feel like a broken record but there's no other option. We can either not talk about them at all or we can talk about them and remember them, which also means to miss them and wish they were here. This year I am, again, much more ticked off than in years past (last year I think was the most pissed off year, but I could be forgetting).

Sam: Yes. Always and Forever definitely pretty much sucks. Totally. And forever. BAH! That's such a long darn time!!! I also agree that last year was your 'most pissed off' one...you're only 'ticked' so far. Maybe that's a good thing? Have you considered making a list of the reasons your pissed/ticked? Sometimes, that's therapeutic. (And I'd like to read them! And agree with them!) It seems to me that if I dug up the journal I wrote in the days immediately after Zach's death, I'd find a "pissed off list." I've written them for other things, too. It's helpful to me to acknowledge all the reasons why I'm feeling that way...gives them validity to see them on paper...even if I never look at them after writing it.

Me: I write a lot, but I've never made a list per se. Sounds like a good idea.

Sam: Of course it's a good idea. I came up with it! :-P

Me: I'm ticked because:

- Forever is a long fucking time to live without my baby.
- Forever is a long fucking time to miss my baby.

Sam: True story -- when I read this the first time, I laughed out loud. Because I thought you wrote the same sentence twice & I agree! (And it IS worthy of saying twice!) Now I see they're different. Bummer... Still valid!

Me: It's not fair to have to live without him (yeah yeah who ever said life was fair but still this is seriously not fair!).

Sam: Cue Role-Reversal. I swear, these are my words... :-)

Me: It sucks that Jaymeson and Jake never got to know him.

Sam: But I think they did know him. They were all there together! (Because I believe that babies are sitting on a shelf in heaven, waiting to make their debut on earth...so they were all there (though Jackson wasn't on the shelf) at the same time. Jackson pushed them OFF the shelf. That's just my 2 cents.)

Me: My heart will never completely heal … I can get on with life because I have to (and yes oftentimes it is very good) but that pain and grief will never go away.

Sam: Nope. And–may I just add that—I've been "happy" for so long (though I did shed a few tears this morning), I'm totally afraid of when what I *know* is just under the surface and comes to the top. It has potential to be a volcanic explosion. I'm not prepared to deal with that. AT. ALL.

Me: It sucks to live with the fear and dread that something will happen to one of my other kids (yeah I know all parents are afraid something will happen to one of their children, but I don't think they feel the heart stopping terror when their child sleeps late or gets sick like we do).

Sam: Yes. And -- when we hear of a story, it all comes flooding back.

Me: I hate feeling like I should take down Jackson's pictures and stop including him on our Christmas Card for the sake of Jayme and Jake. Do I really have to act like he never lived to help them to not have an emotional burden to bear? I really don't know the answer to this, and I'm irritated I have to worry about it at all.

Sam: OMG. Really?? Is his presence really that much of an emotional burden to them? Because I haven't considered taking down Zachary's pictures....and when we move from this house (hopefully this summer), I'm totally putting them back on a wall. He did get 'bumped' from our Christmas card this year, but that's because I have them printed at Portrait Innovations and they don't offer me enough fonts & characters! I think you should take that off your list of crap to worry about. It's their lot in life. Just like they have a loser for a dad.

Shit happens & you deal with it. Lucky for them, this shit happened before they got here...so they have minimal to deal with. (Whoa -- did I say that out loud?? Sam takes on the role of pessimistic/realist. I'm pretty sure this follows the previous role-reversal I mentioned. LOL)

Me: I hate that my innocence was lost and part of me died when he did.

Sam: ME TOO! I miss that old chick. She was good people! I said that last night at dinner with my girlfriends and one said -- but we LOVE the New Sam! Yeah. Well....I'm not so much of a fan. I mean, she's all right and all, but I liked the previous one better.

Me: I hate that I can't stand to hear people say crap like "God never gives you something you can't handle" or "Everything happens for a reason." I really want to sit them down and explain to them why that is total bullshit.

Sam: NO KIDDING!!!! It takes EVERYTHING in me not to say, "maybe not, but He surely over-estimates my abilities!" and "well, I wouldn't go that far"....and believe me -- most times, I say it. Not even kidding. If they ask, after that, I'll offer my explanation. If not, I'm good with them thinking that I have little Faith.

Me: Well I'm thinking this list need not go on ... at least not right now. It's kinda making me more mad ☹ And I'm realizing the timing might be really bad for you ... sorry!

Sam: Nope. I'm all good. Your list is just like one I wrote years ago. Seriously. (And I am in a SCARY-GOOD place right now. I promise I'm not taking drugs (prescribed or otherwise).... well, except for that pesky antibiotic which has taken my appetite with it. Best diet plan ever! Down 11 pounds! LOL)

What an amazing friend right? I survived without a paid therapist for *years* with Sam's support. She validated my thoughts and feelings and helped me to see where I was worrying about things I didn't need to worry about, like taking Jackson's pictures down.

Even while Growing in Hope, I still felt the well of sadness (and anger) rise inside me. Sometimes it bubbled up and overflowed. When it did, I had someone I could turn to who helped me to know it was normal. And who reassured me I would get past that plunge of emotion and float back to the surface.

Not everyone has a Sam… and that's another reason I'm writing this book. Perhaps I can be that kindred spirit and friend for you through my Grief Companion program. I'm not quite as funny as Sam, but I'm a great listener and encourager. Heck, I wrote this whole book to encourage you… I hope it's working.

Grief Companion Corner: We're Never Really Getting Over it, Are We?

Dear Jennifer,

It's been four years and I still have a hard time talking about my mom to anyone. I went to lunch with a friend and she said something about planting flowers. It made me think of my mom and how we used to plant flowers together and I got choked up. My friend didn't understand why I'm not "over it" yet.

I cry less now but the grief is not subsiding. I'm really struggling with how to move on with my life. I don't know why this is so difficult. I guess I'm just trying to come to terms with the fact that we're never really getting over it, are we?

Yours truly,
—Confused

Dear Confused,

When people seem puzzled as to why I'm still grieving after many years, I tell them if grief wasn't happening to me, I wouldn't understand either. But since my grief is happening to me, I know it's not due to me refusing to "move on" or "get over it."

I'm living and doing the best I can, but I will always grieve that my baby is not here with me. Sometimes I will grieve more intensely than other times but as you said, no, we're never really getting over it.

We'll always get choked up and feel sad at times, like you did hearing about planting flowers. But we can feel loss and still have space in our hearts for the blessings, too. I don't think you need to worry about getting over it or moving on. Just think about moving forward, one step at a time. And bring your mom right along with you.

Love and hugs,
Jennifer

You're Not Forgetting, You're Growing

One day at a leadership conference hosted by Carey Nieuwhof, I had a surprising realization: *There's something beautiful about grief... it never truly ends.* That probably sounds strange, but you'll see what I mean.

Most attendees were pastors and church staff. I was one of few from the non-profit world, so I often explained my work: "I'm Founder and CEO of the Center for Help and Hope. We support women facing major life transitions like divorce, single parenting, unemployment, grief, etc."

When someone expressed interest in my grief work, I'd share a little more. I'd explain how, once the casseroles and calls stop coming, many grieving people can still barely get out of bed... if they can at all. That's when they need support most, which is why I created a text message support service. (See Resources section.)

Many nodded along... until I reached the point where I said it was possible, eventually, to feel more love than pain. That's when I often lost them. One woman confided, "If my pain softens, doesn't that mean I'm forgetting? I never want to do that."

Grief is beautiful because it never ends, reminding us that the love we're afraid to lose wasn't lost. And it never will be.

I reassured her, "The grief decreases, but the love doesn't. The love stays strong and present. Grief still visits, but so does deep connection. And that means we haven't forgotten. Not even close."

The human heart can not only bear grief, it can restore, expand, and transform because of grief. This is something we begin to understand as we're Growing in Hope.

Grief is beautiful because it never ends, reminding us that the love we're afraid to lose wasn't lost. And it never will be.

Hard Candy Christmas: Sorrow Won't Bring Me Way Down

Seven years after Jackson's death, I wrote the journal entry below. I didn't learn about grief "recovery" for another ten years. But I managed to find a ray of hope in a favorite old song.

December 10, 2010

I've always loved the song Hard Candy Christmas. I grew up in the 70's listening to my dad's favorite songs, and Dolly Parton was one of his favorite entertainers. For one, she had "big jugs" which my dad deeply appreciated. But she was also an amazing singer/songwriter.

We had a jukebox in our TV room so I didn't have to wait for the holidays to hear this song on the radio. I'd punch in the numbers to my favorites and then sing along while I cleaned house.

Even though I've always loved this song and felt the bittersweet emotions it was written to evoke, ever since Jackson died, this song turns me into a sobbing puddle of mush. I can't even sing along because I cry too hard, my voice cracking.

I don't love the feeling of pain, but I do love remembering my beautiful baby boy. This song brings him back to me. And reminds me of all the times I put on a brave face and pretended I was "fine and dandy" when really, inside, I wasn't.

But, as the song says, even when "I'm barely gettin' through tomorrow, still I won't let sorrow bring me way down."

Many people carry around the kind of pain Dolly sings about, and they're never honestly *fine*.

As *The Grief Recovery Handbook* states, "The danger of 'I'm fine' is that it does not help the broken heart. Saying 'I'm fine' merely distracts us and others, while pain and loneliness persist on the inside."

Many people don't know they don't have to live that way. That they can unburden their hearts and live joyful lives no matter what they grieve.

This is a big part of why I write… to let people know they can experience soul-healing recovery after loss. I fundamentally believe in not letting sorrow bring me *too* far down. Yes, sorrow is there. I can't deny it, and I don't want to. But I also don't want to let it get the best of me. You can sense that resolve and resilience in the final sentences of the journal entry. Hope continued to grow and carry me forward.

Life and Death Lessons

On Jackson's eighteenth birthday, in 2021, I took flowers to the cemetery. It was a gorgeous spring day… the vibrant blue sky was dashed with wispy clouds. I cleaned up his space, removing the faded Christmas bouquets and replacing them with bundles of blue hydrangeas, white tulips, and purple hyacinths.

I took a long walk around the grounds. It was peaceful and healing. There was a "birthday party" going on nearby in Babyland, so I didn't linger at his grave.

That evening, I made spaghetti with meat sauce and garlic bread. After eating we settled into the living room to watch *Paul Blart Mall Cop* for movie night. I served mini-bundt cakes for dessert, lemon for me and double-chocolate for the kids. Jayme paused mid-bite and asked, "Hey, Mom. Why are we having bundt cake?"

"Because it's March 7th." She was distracted, cuddling with her boyfriend, and didn't connect the dots.

Midway through the movie, Jayme got a text to go look on the front porch. She came in with a paper wrapped bundle of yellow and purple flowers and a "Happy Birthday!" balloon. She was confused and asked, "Whose birthday is it?"

I said, "Jackson's…"

Later, after everyone had gone to bed, the dog started barking. I got up to find him upset with the balloon floating near his kennel. As I was moving it out of sight, Jamye came into the kitchen. She too wanted to know what spooked the dog. I said, "He was probably thinking, 'Hey, that floating thing is *not* supposed to be here.'" We laughed.

Then Jayme's face grew serious, "Mommy, I'm sorry. I know about Jackson's birthday (and death day), but I don't know the exact dates…"

"It's okay, hon," I said. "I'm glad you don't worry about the dates. You don't need to."

"I just feel bad. I hope he's not mad at me." I assured her he wasn't mad at her, and neither was I. She continued, "One day we'll get to see what he would've looked like."

"He'd be eighteen now," I said.

"Yeah," Jayme said. "He would be getting a real driver's license, not a provisional one. He could take me shopping. He'd tell my boyfriend, 'Hey, man. You better take care of my sister.' That would've been cool." We hugged, and she did her little circular finger massage thing on my back… so sweet.

She went back to bed, and I tried to concentrate on my book - *Atomic Habits* by James Clear. Then I started thinking about Jayme feeling bad about not remembering Jackson's birthday. I wish I'd said more to reassure her, something like this:

I'm glad you don't feel the need to keep up with 'the dates.' This isn't your burden to bear. It's mine. Someday you'll have your own burden to bear.

When your time comes, I hope I will have taught you that even when some things are so desperately awful, there are still so many amazing gifts and blessings. A blessing doesn't erase a hurt. But we can't let the hurt blind us to the blessing.

Probably, even if I *had* said all this, these are lessons Jayme will have to learn on her own.

Conclusion

The more hope I let myself feel, the more I embraced the truth I wish I'd expressed to Jayme: *A blessing doesn't erase a hurt.*

Blessings don't cancel the pain of loss. And in fact, canceling pain would be a mistake. Because pain has power. Pain can propel you to learn what once seemed impossible… that you have the ability to do more than survive trauma and tragedy.

You can rise.

You can recalibrate.

You can rebuild.

And emerge fully restored and gloriously alive.

This kind of life isn't found on the easy road. It's found when you choose the road less traveled. And as you continue down the road, grief and gratitude begin to walk side by side, each making room for the other. This signals the shift toward the next G – Grateful.

EIGHT

THE 5TH G: GRATEFUL

Many grievers believe if they can just make sense of their loss, they'll automatically reach a sense of closure. We go over and over the death, excavating every tiny thing that happened (or didn't happen) with a fine-toothed comb. I wrote about this in my journal 6 months after Jackson died.

September 6, 2003:

Sometimes my brain spins around and around trying to come up with some way to make all this be a bad dream. I replay the time I had with Jackson, and I think about any and all things I could have done differently, hoping that I can rewrite history. It's crazy. It's pointless. But I keep doing it.

No matter the mental gymnastics, we often come up empty-handed and confused. I never could make sense of, or find meaning in, my three-month-old baby dying. An awful, tragic thing happened.

For a long time, I thought meaning would come from finding answers or making sense of what happened. Later I realized I was searching in the wrong place.

David Kessler discussed this struggle with Brené Brown on her *Unlocking Us* podcast (March 31, 2020).[8] He shared so many golden nuggets that Brown spent most of the interview saying, "Oh my God! Can you say that again?"

Meaning and purpose aren't found in death. They're found in life.

Among the many insights he shared, two stood out:

1. You can't use the idea of 'finding meaning' to avoid the pain of grief. Kessler said, "You're going to be in pain… There's no way around the pain... Meaning will be the cushion, but you've got to feel the pain."
2. People also get stuck because they can't find meaning in the death of a loved one. People say, "My loved one was murdered; there's no meaning in that." Or "My loved one died of cancer or Alzheimer's; there's no meaning." But Kessler points out they're looking for meaning in the wrong place.

Meaning and purpose aren't found in death. They're found in *life*. In your loved one's life *and* what you choose to do with your life after loss.

Reflecting on life and looking for every big and small thing we're grateful for, instead of what we missed, is the pathway to find the meaning we seek.

Answering a Thirteen-Year Question

On Tuesday, June 3, 2003, the sun was setting. I sat on my bedroom floor, legs criss-crossed. I tapped my best friend's number into the cordless phone. I was calling to tell her the unfathomable news… that Jackson went down for a nap at the babysitter's house that afternoon. And never woke up.

She screamed, "Oh my gosh! Oh my gosh! Jennifer, what can I do?" Then, she said something so mind-bendingly confusing: "Jennifer, Jackson fulfilled his purpose. He served the purpose God created him for."

I don't know what I said but I know what I was thinking, *"How? How can that be true?"* The question haunted me for years. How could a three-month-old baby fulfill his purpose? How could God have intended for him to live such a short time? *It made no sense.*

That question stayed with me for thirteen years. The answer finally came in 2016 during life coach training. Our instructor, Diana, led us through a visualization exercise designed for us to discover our life's purpose. After some breathwork, she asked us to imagine ourselves somewhere peaceful and relaxing.

I found myself sitting in the white sand on a deserted beach. The sky was a deep chambray blue with a line of cottony clouds above the horizon. The water sparkled, and the waves swooshed. The air smelled deliciously salty. Deeper into the meditation, a path leading away from the beach came into view. I stood up, wiped at the sand on my shorts, and headed down the path, through a thicket of tall spruce trees.

The next step was to discover a sanctuary. I came to a clearing in the trees and saw an old church. The weathered door made no sound as I entered. An orange carpet-runner led me down the aisle.

The instructor said, "You are greeted by your guide."

My guide was next to the podium... it was my baby Jackson. He was sitting in his neon blue bouncy seat. I knelt down and asked him, "What is my life purpose?"

He answered, not in words, but I heard him in my mind:

Mom, you're already fulfilling your purpose by taking such great care of Jaymeson and Jake. And now you're pursuing this new career of life coaching and helping people in need. You're doing so good, Mom. I'm proud of you. Just keep doing what you're doing.

Then, he flashed me one of his 1000 kilowatt smiles. My heart swelled with pure joy.

The instructor prompted, "Now, say goodbye to your guide, knowing they're always with you."

I set off, through the spruce trees, returning to the beach. The instructor called us back to the classroom. I opened my eyes and relaxed into the sensation of my heart, soothed and peaceful. I was on the right path. My son was okay. He was proud of me.

And I had an answer to my 13-year-long question: Did Jackson fulfill his purpose?

Yes. He fulfilled the purpose of being the unique and wonderful soul God created him to be. As my guide, his beautiful soul led me to *my* purpose.

Loving Jackson and losing him altered my fundamental being and pushed me onto an unwanted divergent path. But I'm grateful that I've come to learn more about life and purpose than I ever could have if not for him.

Grief Companion Corner: Is This Normal?

Dear Jennifer,

I was looking through pictures this morning, and after five years it just hit me all over again that my husband is gone, and I won't see him again until I die. I'm on the verge of tears. I feel like I'm not "supposed" to be sad anymore but I can't help it. Is this normal? What can I do to feel better?

—Unsure

Dear Unsure,

Yes, getting hit with the harsh reality all over again is normal. The pictures were probably the trigger… realizing there will never be any more pictures other than the ones you have. These sudden bursts of sadness will happen. Take the time you need to feel and recover. Acknowledging your sad feelings is important. Accept your sadness as part of you, and know it will accompany you throughout your grief journey.

As to what you can do to feel better, I offer some advice from a favorite historical fiction author (Ginny Dye): "Let the splendor of the universe soften the reality of life."

There are many mini-splendors that can soften pain and soothe your spirit:

- Birds chirping outside your window as you stretch and get ready for the day.
- Rain falling heavily on the roof while you're safe and dry and warm inside.
- The smell of your morning coffee, the taste and the warmth, as you sip from a favorite mug.
- A quiet walk in the woods or around the block in your neighborhood.

- A long, tender hug.

Notice the small splendors, gifts from the universe, and let them comfort and bolster you.

Love and hugs,
Jennifer

Laughs and Lessons from a Hospital Room

When we go through loss, our purpose can be magnified if we focus on what we're grateful for, even when things are scary. This is how we become stronger and more resilient through our grief transformation, which bridges from the 5th G, Grateful to the 6th G, Glorious. I experienced this one weekend, beginning with a frantic call from my mom.

"Jennifer, I'm having chest pains," she said. Her usually authoritative voice quivered with fear. "They're radiating down to my stomach." She whispered those last words, and I struggled to hear them.

"For how long?" I asked.

"All afternoon," she moaned. She was so scared because this was how her mom died — with these very symptoms of a heart attack. "I don't know what to do."

I said, "I'm calling 911. You take an aspirin and sit down. I'll be right there."

The paramedics arrived shortly after I did. Four young, good-looking paramedics quickly loaded her onto a stretcher and wheeled her out the front door. I stood beside the ambulance waiting as they loaded her. Mom called, "Bring my purse!"

"I have your ID and insurance cards," I said. She said again, "Bring my purse!"

What is it with old ladies and their purses? They show up to every gathering clutching a big, black handbag that weighs as much as a house cat. You offer to take it, and they say, "No, thank you. I'll just hold on to it." Then they sit with it in their lap the rest of the day. *Weird.* And here was my mom delaying the ambulance because she wasn't leaving without her purse. The thought made me laugh and I was grateful for a moment of levity in the midst of chaos.

That night was an ordeal. At least Mom was moved out of the ER quickly and up to a room where they began treatment, not for a heart attack, but a blockage in her intestines. I sat waiting in a stiff metal chair as the air conditioner hissed and the IV machine beeped every 15 seconds. Heavy doors thunked down the hallway. Voices drifted in and out… some muffled, others obnoxiously loud for a place full of sick people trying to rest and the time being almost midnight.

Mom was finally asleep thanks to the morphine. She wore her traditional sleeping face, a deeply downturned frown. Mine is the same. It's so strikingly unattractive that I try *really* hard not to fall asleep in public places (airplanes, hospital waiting rooms, on the couch after holiday meals of ham and sweet potato casserole).

Soon she stirred and, feeling much better, wanted to have a chat. It felt like any other night at her house, sitting in the living room, with *Golden Girls* on TV in the background, and Cindy jumping from the recliner over to me on the couch for a belly rub, then back to Mom.

The subject quickly turned to my dad. She said, "He made me laugh so much. About a thousand times a day, even when he was sick." Her eyes teared up as she told me she still missed him terribly.

I said, "Yeah, I still miss Jackson even after twenty years. It's really hard when you lose someone, and people expect that one day you'll magically be 'over it.' It just doesn't work like that."

"No, it doesn't," she agreed.

I paused, then admitted, "If I hadn't lost Jackson, I can see myself being one of 'those people' who think it's strange and possibly unhealthy for someone to still cry and miss their baby who died so many years ago. I never could've understood how you feel if that hadn't happened to me."

Conclusion

As I watched her sleep, I was grateful for the unexpected gift my grief allowed me to give my mom that night: complete understanding and empathy.

When you've walked through loss, no explanation is needed. When you haven't, no explanation will ever be enough.

That's why the grief recovery journey I share in Chapters 10 and 11 is so transformative. It's not just about remembering or reflecting. It's about sharing your story from a place of raw honesty and hard-won gratitude, with someone who can truly witness and receive it.

When that happens, your healing deepens. And you discover your loved one's life doesn't just live on in you. It ripples outward, impacting and uplifting others along the way.

And that feels downright Glorious.

When you've walked through loss, no explanation is needed. When you haven't, no explanation will ever be enough.

If Not For Him

If not for him, I wouldn't be me.
I wouldn't be a mom of three.
I wouldn't have learned the lessons living without him taught me.
I wouldn't understand the depths of grief.
I wouldn't revel in the boundless gifts of hope and love.
I wouldn't have a transformed spirit and soul.

– Jennifer Hacker (September, 2024)

Nine

The 6th G: Glorious

For years, I believed I could never fully recover from the death of my son. Sure, I had worked to find healing and felt genuinely content most of the time. And I experienced incredible joy in my two beautiful children who came after. But still, I thought I'd always be at least somewhat broken.

I mean, you can't be whole again when a vital piece of you has been carved out of your body and your life. *Can you?*

Actually yes, if you do the work, you can feel whole again. Your light, once nearly lost in grief, can be reignited, allowing you to shine with courage and confidence.

Better Than Before

My first glimpse of Glorious emerged in the fall of 2018. I was working on my vision board, flipping through *People* magazines searching for inspirational pictures and headlines. An article about kintsugi caught my eye.

I'd heard of it before and didn't find it especially impactful. But on this day, the unique method of repairing broken pottery left me feeling inspired. The artisans don't simply glue the pieces back together and try to hide the damage. They highlight the cracks, turning them from flaws into the piece's most beautiful feature.

Suddenly, sitting in the middle of my living room floor, surrounded by magazines, scissors, glue dots… I believed my broken pieces actually could come together, and my future self could be *better* than the me who died when my son did. I had more hope for the future than I'd had in a very long time.

I was excited to share this with my coach Diana in our next session. I said, "Last week when I was working on my vision board, I read an article about kintsugi. Have you heard of it?"

"No, tell me about it."

I paced back and forth across my office as I explained what I learned: *"Kintsugi is the Japanese art of repairing broken pottery."* I stepped from my oversized desk and the towering ficus tree in the corner.

With my next breath, my voice caught in my throat. I stopped in front of the window, trying to collect myself. I could feel the dreaded lump at the back of my throat and decided not to hold back the tears. I let them stream down my cheeks as I crossed the burgundy rug.

My words quickening, I continued, "Artisans collect the broken pieces but when they go to work, they use a special method to rejoin them… they fill the cracks with *gold*. Using a valuable material turns the seeming 'imperfections' into beauty marks. When they're done, a pile of shattered pieces is made whole. Not just restored, but radiant."

My coach said, "Jennifer, this is amazing. I hear you getting choked up. Tell me about this emotion."

I fumbled my words, still crying. "I just… I never knew. I never knew for sure if I would ever be whole or feel whole again. Somehow, learning about kintsugi made me believe I can. I don't know *how* yet, but I know I will. And it's going to make a difference for more people."

My coach and I celebrated in the wonder of this breakthrough. Of course, that doesn't mean everything changed then and there simply by having this new knowledge. But this was the turning point. For the first time, I felt sure I wasn't stuck at mile-marker "Good Enough." I was on the path to transformation.

I'd always believed losing my old self was an additional loss, stacked on top of the loss of Jackson. The lightbulb that came on when I learned about kintsugi changed that.

My motto became, "I'm not going back to who I was. I'm not supposed to. I'm changing into something even better." Kintsugi gave me a glimpse into the future. My brokenness was a part of me; shattered yet able to be mended. Now my pieces were ready to be assembled… for a glorious purpose.

As I kept walking my own healing path, I realized something else. I could guide others toward the same hope and possibility I found.

You *can* heal. You can feel soul-deep joy. You can be *whole again*. Not as the person you once were, but as a gold-filled masterpiece: reforged, resilient, and radiant.

Redemption

One of the most helpful books I read in my early grief was *When Bad Things Happen to Good People* by Harold Kushner. His son died from Progeria (rapid aging disease). I learned from Kushner that at some point, we must stop asking "Why did this happen to me?" and start asking, "What can I do now?" In other words, we come to terms with the loss by *doing* something to redeem it.

Regardless of why you think bad things happen in life, whether you agree or disagree that God is responsible, a critical element to surviving and healing is to learn how to make something meaningful from the pain.

Now, if you're thinking, *"How in the world would I do that? I don't think I can"*... that's okay. There's no rush.

If you're still in the early periods of grief (Gutted, Grinding, and even Gaining Momentum), not wanting to feel better is perfectly natural. You may worry that healing is a betrayal or that you're forgetting your loved one. I felt the same way.

Inspired by Kushner's book, I spent years working to redeem the loss of my son, in small and big ways, taking my time as life circumstances and my emotional capacity allowed.

Remaining broken doesn't change the past, but healing can change the future.

Through trial and error, I learned how to survive, and even how to find a solid feeling of happiness, as you read in Chapter 7. During my Grateful period, I became more emotionally present with my children and family. In time, I began to seek the next iteration of growth asking, "What more can I do to redeem the pain and honor my son's life?"

As I shared in Chapter 5, grief never truly ends, and neither does love. However, we can choose to tip the scales toward love. As Kushner writes:

"Pain makes some people bitter and envious. It makes others sensitive and compassionate. It is the result, not the cause, of pain that makes some experiences of pain meaningful and others empty and destructive."

Here's an example of the contrast Kushner describes. In the *Harry Potter* series, Severus Snape lives a lonely life due to his unrequited love for Harry's mother. Instead of letting his pain turn him into the bitter, evil man he pretends to be, he chooses to protect Harry, even at great personal risk. Snape's redemption comes through years of secret acts of bravery and kindness. Snape transformed his pain into loyalty and selfless protection.

Twelve years after Jackson's death, my life changed in a way I never imagined. I discovered my compulsion to help others wasn't just a coping mechanism… it was a calling. My first big step toward redemption was founding a non-profit organization, the Center for Help and Hope, to support women facing major life transitions. The next step was leaving my corporate finance career to become a Certified Life Coach and Grief Specialist. In the process of learning how to support others, I experienced my glorious transformation.

But don't worry, you don't have to make a dramatic change to redeem your pain. Maybe you commit to being a better parent, a more loving and understanding spouse, or a more compassionate friend. Or maybe you start a scholarship fund in memory of your loved one, or volunteer for a cause they cared about.

Remaining broken doesn't change the past, but healing can change the future. Let this truth be an anchor, as you hold your broken heart together, allow it to grow stronger, and seek your own path to redemption.

I hope you'll choose a path that leads you, not into bitterness, but into *betterness*. (I know it's not a real word, but it fits).

Saying "Yes" to the Craziest Things

My kids had wanted a pet *forever*. I'd always vigorously said, "No way. I *cannot* be responsible for *any* additional living things. Not even a goldfish. Not even a plant!"

Throughout my Gaining Momentum, Growing in Hope, and even Grateful periods, I didn't budge. But that didn't stop them from asking.

One day in 2020, they brought up the subject of a pet again. And to everyone's surprise, especially mine, I didn't immediately say, "No!" Instead I said, "I'll think about it." And I found myself coming around to the idea: *Maybe a pet wouldn't be the worst idea after all.*

Not long after that shift, my daughter Jayme made an even bigger ask. She said, "Mom, let's get a foreign exchange student."

I was dumbfounded. "What on earth? Why?" I asked.

"Last year my friend, Genevieve, hosted Carmen from Colombia, and they were best friends," she gushed. "And they still keep in touch to this day. I want that. I want a sister!"

Oof. She got me with the sister stuff. I have two incredible sisters, and I'd always wished I had more kids, at least one more so Jayme could have a sister. Of course, I didn't say yes right away. I said I would think and pray about it.

Not long after, Jayme came flying through the front door, slamming it shut with the heel of her tennis shoe, plopping her backpack on the hall table, and rushing to the living room to exclaim, "Mom, we *need* to meet with the PAX coordinator. They have a bunch of kids who don't have host families yet, and we're running out of time!"

The exchange student idea would've been dead in the water, except that prior to the topic coming up, I had a sudden and strange desire to clean out the spare bedroom. The official junk room was piled high with books, clothes, photo albums, boxes, *stuff*. I'd already cleaned out most of the junk when Jayme brought up hosting an exchange student. Soooooo, I know you see where this is headed.

We met with the coordinator, and as we looked through the

student profiles, the perfect girl came up—Elise. Her letter grabbed us immediately. She wrote about being a hard worker, having a close loving family, caring about doing a good job, being respectful… everything you'd want a stranger to say if they were coming to live with you for ten months. But she sounded genuine, not pretending to be great just to be chosen.

And the rest is history. Elise arrived nine weeks later, two weeks after Orion, our Havanese puppy. Now that's the gift of transformation: I went from saying no to a goldfish and a plant to saying yes to a dog and a *daughter*.

Grief Floats

Hitting the milestone of opening our home was just one step on the journey of a thousand miles. I passed another one more privately. As you've read a few times in these pages, music and certain songs used to force me to acknowledge and feel my deep pain. But over time, music has become mostly a comfort, something that soothes my soul and makes me feel closer to Jackson, not farther apart.

One night I was up late when a song lyric popped into my mind, sudden and clear. With it came a rush of Jackson's nearness, gifting me with a magical moment. I opened my journal and wrote:

JULY 2020

"A breath away's not far to where you are."
This line from a song by Josh Groban pops into my head out of nowhere.
It brings me so much comfort.
My sweet boy is just right here, a breath away from me.
We are close. We are together.
I cling to this thought and feel its truth.
It heals me.
It's painful while also being positively powerful.
My heart hurts and expands in the very same moment in time.

*But love triumphs over the pain... It fills me with
Purpose, gratitude, depth of understanding, hope,
and inexplicable joy.*

*How can you feel true joy in the midst of pain and loss?
Through beautiful memories of ordinary mo-
ments in time,
Like sudden magical smiles.
And heart-wrenching times when you stay up
all night,
Weathering the storm, waking up in the morn-
ing happy,
And 100% appreciating the here and now.
Not worried about or even remembering last
night's struggle.*

*Love conquers all. It bears all. It is everlasting.
I breathe in deeply and feel love surrounding me.
My love for Jackson. His love for me.
And God revealing himself and the depth of his love
for all of humanity.
For, we are His children. Never to be forgotten. Never
to be forsaken.
He treasures those sudden magical smiles... just as I do.
Wow.*

Grief Companion Corner: Is It True Our Loved Ones Are Always With Us?

Dear Jennifer,

My son died 2 months ago. A friend tried to comfort me and convince me that our loved ones are always with us. She said if we could only see in that realm, we would know. Do you believe this? I want to believe this.

—Hoping It's True

Dear Hoping It's True,

Yes, I absolutely believe this. I believe Jackson is with me, every-where and all the time. I feel his presence.

I know it hurts so bad in the first few months. For me, months 4 - 6 were the worst. So don't think you're going crazy if you start to feel worse before you start to feel better.

After about 8 months, I actually felt good some of the time. I know you will get there too. I see happiness and joy in your future and I don't mean 5 or 10 years from now, relatively soon all things considered. You don't have to rush to get there though. Take your time and honor your feelings.

In the meantime, I hope it comforts you to know: I believe your son is with you now and he always will be.

Love and hugs,
Jennifer

My poem and the words of advice shared with "Hoping It's True" brought to mind another recent *wow* moment.

I was talking with my friend Hannah about how much I want to finish this book even though it means I'll have to put myself "out there" and thus feel exposed and vulnerable.

I said to Hannah, "I don't want to be in front. I don't dream of stages or spotlights. But I do want people who feel hopeless to find hope. I want people who feel broken to know that brokenness is abso-lutely real, yet temporary. I want grievers to know they can feel whole again. I want those who think they're crazy for feeling tremendous sadness after two decades (or more) to know it's natural, even though most people will say otherwise. We still love after twenty years, so why wouldn't we feel sad and miss that person sometimes too?"

Hannah lost her grandpa "Pops" several years ago and still feels the pain of that loss deeply. So she was nodding along in complete understanding.

Encouraged, I kept going, "What I *really* want people to know is this: after you do the work to transform grief and release pain, you still plunge into moments of sadness (maybe triggered by a song, a smell, or a sunset). But in those moments, pain isn't the strongest thing you feel. What you feel most is the overwhelming *presence* of love."

And my brilliant friend perfectly captured the essence of what I was trying to say: "*You feel like you had a visit.*" I nodded yes, both of us with tears in our eyes. Another W.O.W.

C.S. Lewis wrote of a similar experience which he likened to having a "meeting" with his beloved wife:

> "And suddenly, at the very moment when, so far, I mourned H. least, I remembered her best. Indeed it was something (almost) better than memory; an instantaneous, unanswerable impression. To say it was like a meeting would be going too far. Yet there was that in it which tempts one to use those words. It was as though the lifting of the sorrow removed a barrier."

Conclusion

This is the transformation I hope you'll pursue. Where grief once overwhelmed you with absence, it now overwhelms you with presence. Where you once felt only the ache of missing them, instead you feel the salve of loving them and being loved by them.

Today, when I think of Jackson, I feel a subtle bittersweetness, quickly followed by a beautiful burst of love and wonder. This is what lies ahead on the journey from Gutted to Glorious.

TEN

MY GRIEF TRANSFORMATION STORY: PART 1 UNEXPECTED BEGINNING

Perhaps you're thinking: "Moving from Gutted to Glorious sounds tremendous, but how? How does that transformation actually happen?"

The answer isn't convenient or comfortable. As I often tell my clients: "We don't learn and grow from doing what's easy. We learn and grow from doing what's hard." Getting over the hump of doubt and fear to change your home base from Grateful to Glorious requires facing the behemoth wall of pain and, here's the crucial part, letting it go.

It means carrying your love forward with you, not as who you once were, but who you're becoming: renewed, restored, and lit from within by a sacred spark.

For some people, healing is facilitated through modalities like EMDR (Eye Movement Desensitization and Reprocessing) or EFT (Emotional Freedom Techniques, often called "tapping"). For me, the starting point was a Grief Recovery program. It wasn't a one-and-done moment, but it gave me a powerful push in the right direction and a foundation to keep building on. The point isn't which method you land on, but that you engage with something that helps you release pain and reclaim life.

You get to choose which voice will guide you... and shape the rest of your healing journey.

You don't have to see the entire road to take the first step. This chapter and the next share what my journey looked like, not as a prescription, but as proof that transformation is possible.

In *Permission to Mourn*, Tom Zuba describes how choosing to live again after loss is like getting back up on the horse. The struggle to do so stems from two voices doing battle every day in your head. One voice says, "The sorrow is too deep. The loss too great." The other voice says, "You were born to be radiant... Not in spite of the fact that someone you love has died. But because of the fact that someone you love has died."

Can you picture yourself up on that horse? Can you feel what it would be like to live again?

You get to choose which voice will guide you… and shape the rest of your healing journey.

Post-Traumatic Growth

In the mid-1990's, psychologists Richard Tedeschi and Lawrence Calhoun studied the phenomenon of how adversity can lead to unexpected strength. They coined the term for it, Post-Traumatic Growth (PTG). PTG is a positive mental shift experienced as a result of trauma/adversity.[9]

Though I didn't learn about PTG until 2023, I intuitively knew this kind of growth was possible because I experienced it, and my clients had, too.

PTG suggests, the time will come when, *because* of your trauma, you'll be able to:

➤ Experience more profound joy, gratitude, and compassion than ever before.
➤ Be fully present and participating in your life.
➤ Have more intimate and meaningful relationships.
➤ View life through a completely changed perspective.
➤ Find a new purpose in life.

This list encapsulates the principle of kintsugi, the Japanese art of repairing broken pottery with gold, which I mentioned in the last chapter. Our grief, whether from death or life-transitions, does change us, and we decide if our change is for the better.

I thought I had healed as much as any parent could after losing a child. After seventeen years, I believed I'd reached the limits of what was possible... that the late-night tears and lingering sadness were simply part of my reality forever.

It took a client drowning in her own grief to show me that deeper healing was possible, and that my most profound transformation was yet to come.

A Life-Changing Encounter

In 2019, a new client, Vicki, signed up to work with me. She wanted to stop being stuck in grief and start living again. Her husband of 30+ years had died four years prior.

In our first meeting I discovered she was still essentially shuttle-running between Gutted, Grinding, and *occasionally* Gaining Momentum. She spent most of her days alternating between sleeping, watching TV, and crying while staring at her husband's picture on the wall. In her first session, she said, "I want to feel better, but how do you do that and not forget?"

It wasn't a surprising question. It's one of grief's FAQ's, though many never say it out loud. *How can I heal and still remember?* The fear of forgetting keeps many grievers stuck for years.

Vicki was a prime example in fact. She'd spent the past four years doing everything she could to remember, ONLY remember. She avoided people and life. *She remembered with determination, believing it was the only way to stay connected to him.*

And yet, there she was sitting in my office, considering the possibility of healing.

Vicki was my first experience coaching someone through grief. Based on everything I'd read, I knew where we needed to begin. She had to tell the story of her husband's death. After four long years, she'd never told a soul what happened.

When she arrived for her next session, she agreed to tell me her grief story.

I began by reading from Tom Zuba's book, *Permission to Mourn*:

I invite you to sit down. In the chair next to me. I will breathe with you. In and out. In and out… So your mind can slow down. And your heartbeat can soften. And your body can begin to release the tension and tightness you have been carrying for such a long long long time. Start wherever you want. At the beginning. The middle. The end. It is okay if you jump around. If you repeat yourself. If you forget some of the details or some of the order and have to go back and start over… I'll let you tell me about the day your life changed. Forever.

Vicki took a deep breath and shared her most sacred memories of her beloved husband, their life together, and the circumstances of his death. It was powerful and emotional for both of us. Afterward, we hugged. I said, "Thank you. I really like seeing you and talking with you."

She replied, "I really like talking to you, too. And I don't normally open up to people, but you're just so easy to talk to."

When Compassion Wasn't Enough

Unfortunately, Vicki attended only a few more sessions, in which I saw that she was still mostly consumed with pain, sadness, anger, bitterness, and fear. Bottom line, she didn't truly want to feel better, at least not more than she wanted to hold onto her pain. Our sessions went something like this:

Me – Friendships was on your list of things to work on. Do you want to make some friends?
Vicki – Yes.
Me – Do you know anyone who is a potential candidate?
Vicki – No.
Me – Do you have any hobbies or places you go where you can meet someone?
Vicki – I went to a few dance classes, but I can't dance, and I got stuck with the same bad partner. Not interested in that anymore.
Me – What about other things you could do, not related to making friends, but just feeling better. Have you tried journaling?
Vicki – In the beginning, I wrote and journaled a LOT.
Me – Did it help?
Vicki – No.
Me – Did you find any routines or practices that did help?
Vicki – No.

For every potential idea (friendships, hobbies, journaling), Vicki had a reason why it wouldn't work or why she'd already tried it without success. Her final response was always the same: "I don't want to do anything. I don't care. My husband is gone."

Even if Vicki had a genuine desire to heal and move forward, I realized I didn't have the right tools to help her. I understood grief. I could listen compassionately. But that wasn't enough for her to have a transformative experience.

This was unacceptable. I needed more tools. More skills. So the next person who came to me in grief could leave not only feeling seen and supported, but also, healed and hopeful.

A Hidden Struggle: My Own Grief

I jumped online and started searching. I found a certification program that looked promising. According to their website, the Grief Recovery Method® was evidence-based, action-based, and had reached tens of millions worldwide. This was it. The perfect program to help me, help Vicki.

I'm sure you noticed… my motivation had nothing to do with me. I thought I was doing fine with my grief. I was working, enjoying my coaching career, and raising two great kids. Overall, life felt good.

But as I confessed in Chapter 5, there were moments, after the kids were in bed, when a book or a scene from an old movie would break through my shell. The pent-up tears would flow, the pain spilling out. I never told anyone about those nights. It was just me and my grief. The deep sadness inside… I thought it was simply how life was after losing your child.

Slow Start

In January of 2020, I attended the Grief Recovery Method® certification program created by John James. He coined the term "grief recovery" and founded The Grief Recovery Institute. James and Russell Friedman co-wrote *The Grief Recovery Handbook*, and we used it like a textbook in the training.

The first day, oh my gosh it was so frustrating. We spent the entire day talking about all the things you and I already know: society is ignorant about grief, people say the dumbest things, grief myths abound, blah, blah, blah.

I didn't like "going around the room" when each person would share personal thoughts and feelings related to the teachings. For example, "What myth about grief did you learn today that surprised you or resonated with you?" or "What hurtful comment or cliché did you hear most often?" I'm sure it was new information and helpful to some classmates, but I was impatient. I wanted to get to the good stuff.

There was one surprising moment though, at the beginning when we were asked, "What loss/losses brought you here?" When it was my turn, I started crying almost immediately and could barely get the words out, "My primary loss is my son, Jackson." And as you know, I do *not* like crying in front of people, *especially* people I don't know. *The intensity of that emotion was my first clue that something deeper was happening.* This wasn't just about learning to help other people. This program was stirring something in me that I'd buried for years.

The deep sadness inside... I thought it was simply how life was after losing your child.

But, anyway, beyond that strange emotional outburst, the first day was a big nothing-burger. I was expecting a juicy bacon cheeseburger of knowledge, and instead I got an overcooked patty on a dry bun. I went home and told my fiancé, "I think I might have wasted a few thousand dollars."

Making Progress: Reviewing a Lifetime of Losses

Thankfully, on the second day, we waded into uncharted waters. The first current we navigated was the "Loss History Graph." In this exercise, we completed a thorough and detailed review of all the loss events in our lives. I learned this is an important step because everyone has unhealed wounds from the past... painful life transitions and challenges that we barely acknowledged and therefore could not have healed from.

This process was especially helpful for me because I spent my life avoiding feelings and being vulnerable; I was raised and conditioned to get over things quickly. Which I did by putting my feelings into a box.

My box was jammed full, ready to burst open and send the feelings flying. I imagine the explosion would look something like those voluminous Hogwarts letters that swirled and hurled around the Dursley's house trying to reach Harry Potter.

To prepare for creating my loss review, I sat in a caramel colored leather chair by the window and brainstormed. I started with my first conscious memory. Around six years old, my dad returned from a business trip, and he brought all us kids a souvenir… mine was a new piggy bank. It was made of semi-translucent green glass in the shape of a pig. We didn't have much money so getting something new when it wasn't my birthday or Christmas was a big deal. I walked down to my best friend Majik's house to show it off.

As I was walking back home, I lost hold of the piggy bank. It hit the pavement and splintered into tiny, irreparable pieces. *I was devastated.* And angry. As I headed home, every time I came to a crack in the sidewalk, I stomped my foot and said, "I hate God!"

From this memory, I let my mind wander, pondering these questions as I wrote:

- What life experiences were extremely painful?
- What life events do I look back on and feel sadness, confusion, anger?
- What do I wish had been different?

For the first time in my life, I paused to acknowledge each loss and the emotions that I'd previously ignored and exiled into "the box."

Until this point, I thought deep healing was only needed for big losses, death-related losses. I also had no idea just *how much* unresolved pain I carried. I had a 28-ton trunk strapped to my back and somehow managed to run through life, smiling, producing, high-functioning… as if the trunk of banished feelings wasn't there.

Wading Into the Scary Waters of Vulnerability

After recording my notes and turning them into a timeline (or "graph" as the instructor called it), the next step was to split into pairs and share with a partner.

Before we began, the instructor explained that the sharing partner should make an effort to describe each event using *feeling* words, rather than citing a history of events. She let us know we might become emotional and we might not. She asked that if we did become emotional, to try our best to push the words up and out and keep walking our way through the timeline.

To the listening partners, she said, "Your job is to be a heart with ears." She continued, "Even though you don't talk, you show your partner you're listening with eye contact and appropriate facial expressions. You can express sadness or surprise where it makes sense with a quiet "oh" or "ahh" but no talking or commentary whatsoever."

As soon as I started sharing my timeline, I forgot the instructions ("use *feeling* words") and instead went into TV news reporter mode, focused on details and facts. Here's an example:

> When I was in fourth grade my parents moved from the city to the country, and I had to change schools. I was the new kid. Then in seventh grade my best friend decided not to be my best friend anymore. With my crispy feathered bangs and hand-me-down clothes, I had to find someone new to hang out with.

See how this narrative is just a chronology of events? Nowhere do I mention a single *feeling*.

I shared my timeline in a detached way, partly because my partner EdRicardo went first, and that's what he did. Since he was there for work, not to sort through a personal loss, that made sense. Still, instead of stepping out of my comfort zone and sharing my *feelings*, I defaulted to reporting dates and events.

As I spoke, I noticed many participants in other groups were extremely emotional. Not that crying is necessary to achieve results. The instructor had said some people cry, some don't. But I thought this was a clue we probably weren't getting as much out of the exercise as we could have. Healing comes from feeling, and I missed this opportunity. Even still, the exercise was worthwhile.

Here's an example of how I could have shared my story differently using feeling words (in italics).

> The summer before fourth grade, my parents moved to the country, and I had to change schools. This was really *hard*. I was *mad* because I thought it was all my brother's fault. And being the new kid made me feel so *anxious and scared and worried* about not fitting in. I did make friends but then in seventh grade, my best friend started hanging out with another group, and that was it. We weren't friends anymore. I felt so *lonely*. And *confused*. I never knew what happened—why she gave up on me and our friendship. Was it my bad hair or my old clothes? I felt *abandoned and not good enough*.

Many trainees were surprised, not only by strong emotions surfacing, but also in identifying multiple short-term coping mechanisms they habitually relied upon when experiencing difficult life and loss events. I, of course, put painful experiences and emotions to the side and concentrated on work and responsibilities. But classmates mentioned all sorts of other things like watching TV day and night, alcohol, drugs, sex, food, sleep, exercise, working, shopping, and more.

Identifying these habits is important because we can change them if they hinder our ability to function. Even more important than knowing which habits to watch out for is being able to let go of guilt (which we'll go into more in Chapter 12).

In Gutted and Grinding, we sometimes need an escape. I'm sure there were times when the escape you chose was not especially healthy. If so, please give yourself grace. When you're suffering intensely, you're not going to make the best choices. Thus, please try not to feel guilty for any bad choices you made when you were doing the best you could to survive the most traumatic times of your life.

Reviewing your history of losses also helps you pinpoint behavior patterns that originated in childhood, and perhaps served you then, but are likely no longer serving you (and may in fact be hurting you) as an adult. You may also discover relationship and environmental factors that impacted you adversely that you subconsciously carried into future relationships.

For example, I discovered my tendency to want to keep the peace came from growing up with a temperamental father. I felt nervous he might erupt at any time. I did whatever I could to keep the peace and avoid his angry outbursts. This set me up for several terrible choices in men and tolerating a whole lot of bad behavior. That said, I'm not blaming my dad or avoiding responsibility for my own decisions. But the dynamic of our relationship and the environment I grew up in did impact my future choices. And it was extremely helpful for me to realize this.

Even though I didn't follow the instructions perfectly, the exercise was an eye-opening lesson. And there was more to come.

Loss Inventory / Review

Approx Year or Age	Brief Description of Event	Long Term Impact 1-10	Coping Mechanisms
4	First memory - Broken piggy bank - I hate God		
whole childhood	Dad angry, hot-tempered	8	Keep the peace
4th grade	Moved to the country. No friends. Didn't fit in.	4	Blend in or be funny
mostly in high school	Fights between brother and dad - lot of anxiety and fear	7	Keep the peace
18	Car accident. Broken neck. Moved home. Lost scholarship	6	
23	Divorce. Moved to SA. Left BF.	5	
94/95	Abusive dating relationship	7	Avoid conflict
99/03	Marriage problems	6	Tolerate
2003	Jackson died	10	Work
2008	Ongoing marital problems / eventual divorce / custody issues	6	Work
06-Cur	Jake / undiagnosed developmental disorder / yrs of stress and confusion	8	Research!
2015	Dad died	3	

Conclusion

The thought of diving into these deep emotional waters can be daunting. But I hope you'll consider doing the work so you can heal your broken heart and live with renewed energy, improved perspective, and the promise of joy.

To heal your unresolved wounds, you must move from passive acceptance of pain to active pursuit of healing.

If you're feeling it isn't fair that you have to do this work, you're right. But being a victim won't lead you to a Glorious life. As *The Grief Recovery Handbook* says, "We have been falsely socialized to believe that we are victims of events and helpless in our response to those events, as well as to the thoughts, feelings, and actions of others."

To heal your unresolved wounds, you must move from passive acceptance of pain (with thoughts like "what's done is done" or "it's not my fault") to active pursuit of healing. You may indeed be a victim of an unfair tragedy or trauma, yet ultimately, you are responsible for your future happiness, and therefore your grief transformation.

The work is hard, but the promise of joy makes every effort worthwhile. As the poet Kahlil Gibran reminds us:

"The deeper that sorrow carves into your being, the more joy you can contain."

Eleven

My Grief Transformation Story: Part 2 Reconciliation

In the afternoon on day two, we chose a specific loss to review in detail. Many people in the class knew right away which relationship felt the most pressing, the most complicated, and the most unresolved. Others needed a bit of time deciding because they had multiple losses still causing them a great deal of pain.

When we lose a close relationship, whether a loved one or a not-so-loved-one, there are always things we wish had been different. There are always unrealized hopes, dreams, and expectations for the relationship that linger. There are also always things you felt but never expressed.

As I contemplated which relationship to choose, I remembered a particularly difficult incident when I'd taken my dad for a 'routine' doctor visit that quickly went south. The doctor took one brief look and said, "The bone is infected, and you'll probably lose your leg." We went directly to the hospital with this dire prognosis.

Normally there would've been multiple family members to help out with hospital duty but not this time. Mom had pneumonia and was home-bound. My older sister was in Europe. My little sister was ten months pregnant. My brothers were working and coming by when they could.

So largely, it was just me and my dad. And let me tell you my dad is *high* maintenance even on his good days. You can't imagine how ridiculous he was when sick. Or perhaps you can if you have a man in your life who reverts to being as needy as a child if his temperature goes up to 99.8. Anyway, back to my dad.

He needed constant attention… his pillow adjusted, the bed adjusted, the TV volume turned up, the TV channel changed, his pain meds increased, socks on, socks off. He refused the regular meals and sent me in search of cookies and pudding. For several hours he discussed and delighted in the idea of taking his amputated leg home to have it stuffed and mounted on the wall!

He got hot and repeatedly took off his gown and lay naked for every unsuspecting nurse, doctor, and visitor to see. The nurses were extremely displeased. They told him, "Sir, you have to leave your gown on." He continued to take it off. After many scoldings, my dad pulled the gown up to his neck and wore it like a fluffy faded blue scarf. Then when the nurses came in, he smiled mischievously and said, "It's still on!"

Once the reality of amputation set in, my dad became depressed. He talked at length about the loss. He wondered how he would get around, how he would drive, how he would take basic care of himself. This made sense.

But after several days I finally said, "Dad, I understand you don't want to lose your leg. Of course you don't. But in this case I think you've got to look at it differently. It's like a breast. Breasts are great; people love breasts. But when they're cancerous and trying to kill you, you have to get rid of them."

He didn't appreciate my analogy. It was too soon. He was still mourning the loss of his leg. He couldn't yet embrace the concept of getting rid of it even for the benefit of staying alive.

At the end of the 4th day, as I was finally leaving to go home to my kids, I stood at the foot of Dad's hospital bed. He said, "You know Jenni, I would have called anyone else to help me. I would have called Mitch or Kay, or Billy or James. But, I'm glad you came."

I cried all the way home. To work so hard and be told the preferred family member was *anyone* but you... it was a knife to my heart. For a long time, I didn't think about what my dad said. I put it in the box to deal with some other time. Unfortunately, time seemed to run out when he died a year later, on my birthday of all days. But as I learned in the training, it's never too late. So for the relationship exercise, I opted to work on the relationship with my dad.

Profound Mending of My Soul

I wish I could say I chose to focus on my dad because remembering the pain of the hospital incident caused me to understand there was much to uncover and unpack about our relationship. But the real truth is, as I confessed in Chapter 1, I went with my dad because I thought it would be easier than talking about the death of my baby. I also believed I stood a good chance of not crying, at least not too much—hah!

One additional factor in choosing my dad was learning the importance of *foundational relationships*. The instructor explained that working on foundational relationships (your mother, your father, the people who raised you) can be the most beneficial. Foundational relationships often have the most "unresolved" elements and longest-term impact on the entirety of who you are, your habits, and your coping mechanisms. Also, when you reconcile foundational relationships, you can experience healing of adjacent relationships as well.

To help us understand this process, our instructor used the analogy of an artichoke. Artichokes have a "heart" deep inside and there are many layers of leaves criss-crossing over the heart. The foundational relationship is the heart of the artichoke. When you reconcile that relationship, many adjacent layers of relationships can be peeled away and healed at the same time.

My relationship with my dad is an example of something most people face... a complex mix of positive and negative memories and feelings. It may seem like the opportunity to resolve the conflicting feelings was lost when he died.

What I came to understand in the next exercise is that you can resolve and "complete" the events that feel painful and unresolved whether your loved one is still alive or has died, and also whether the loss (by divorce, career change, moving, etc.) was recent or long ago.

Completion does *not* mean forgetting your loved one or ending your spiritual connection. The emotional relationship continues.

As *The Grief Recovery Handbook* explains, we're "completing" our "relationship to the pain caused by the loss" and "anything that was left unfinished at the time of the loss."

Essentially, we say the unsaid words and acknowledge our feelings about the things we wish had been different.

With a relationship chosen, we started on our "Relationship Graphs." I sat at a table near the window and reviewed the entire relationship with my dad, remembering and writing down the big moments, negative *and* positive.

Being completely honest and giving attention to the *whole* relationship is important for this activity. When you have a relationship that is/was largely out of balance, there's a tendency to drastically tip the scales to one side or the other, focusing only on the more heavily weighted side.

To achieve healing, you must address both the positive and negative aspects of the relationship. After I selected the fifteen-to-twenty most important relationship events, I drew them out onto a timeline like we did with the loss review. Then, we shared with our partners.

Relationship Review - Dad

| PAINFUL | | | | Yr/Age | POSITIVE | | |
Pattern Created?	Feelings	Impact 1-10	Brief Descrip		Brief Descrip	Impact 1-10	Feelings
				4	First Memory - M&M's and kisses	6	loved, special (PES)
keep the peace, even at the expense of myself	anxiety, fear - later compassion (F, NES)	9	Dad angry, hot-tempered, yelled a lot	4-17			
				4-15	Trips to the beach every summer	8	carefree, safe, happy (PES)
				4-17	Dad worked hard to provide for us	5	ungrateful at the time, grateful later (A, PES)
fly under the radar, be good, don't make dad mad	fear, anxiety (F, NES)	8	Fights between dad and brother	9-12			
	hurt, not special (F, NES)	6	Dad loved sister more	9			
insecure about my body	hurt (F, NES)	6	Comments about my big butt	24			
	embarassed (A, F, NES)	5	Trip to St Croix / Walmart incident	25	St Croix / shopping / pina coladas / bracelet	8	carefree, adventure, fun (PES)
				34	Dad sat with me and let me cry	9	safe (PES)
				35	Dad at Jayme's birth	8	dad's funny (PES)
	frustrated, hurt (F, NES)	8	Dad in hospital / leg amputated / HARD to care for him	45	Bonded during this hard time	6	compassion (PES)
	mad (A, F, NES)	4	Dad died / on my birthday	46			
				48	I missed him	6	love, peace (PES)

Vulnerability Times Two

To begin my turn, I told EdRicardo my first memories of my dad. Like when he returned from business trips, he would bring me M&M's. But to get the M&M's, I had to give him an equal number of kisses. A sweet and treasured memory.

I shared how my dad was angry and temperamental through-out my childhood. I grew up afraid of his outbursts, afraid of con-flict, and determined to keep the peace, even at my own expense. I also learned to "get over things" quickly. There was *no pouting* in our house, unless of course, it was Dad. Those lessons carried into many of my later relationships. Not all, but too many involved volatile or emotionally manipulative men. When they mistreated me, I accept-ed it and moved on. Recognizing this connection doesn't mean my dad was responsible for my choices. It simply helped me understand how the patterns I learned in childhood left me vulnerable to re-peating them.

There were good times, too, though. We went to Port Aransas every summer for family vacations. There were *seven* of us in a pop-up trailer parked on the beach. We didn't have the money to stay at La Quinta, or even Motel 6. But a cramped trailer was still better than being at home, lying around watching Gilligan's Island and the Brady Bunch all day.

I loved to go out into the ocean with Dad. He would sit and read all day, and my siblings and I would pester him to take us out. He'd put us off for hours, but eventually, finally, we'd splash out into the surf. Dad pulled us on rafts, helped us over the waves, and protected us from the really big ones. He was tall and strong, and in those mo-ments, I felt safe and happy to be with him.

As I continued to share all the important moments in the his-tory of my relationship with my dad, I was utterly dumbfounded to find myself and EdRicardo crying. Not a few tears here or there. We were sobbing. I was hardly able to speak at times. EdRicardo sat across from me, taking it all in. Feeling it all with me. His beau-tiful brown eyes overflowed with tears, in sync with mine. I had no idea how much pain was still inside me about my dad until it came pouring out.

The profound mending of my heart and soul that occurred in this moment is best described by Drs. Henry Cloud and John Townsend in *How People Grow*:

"Grief is a relational experience, and your pain has to be seen eye to eye with another person. Someone should be looking at us when we are crying, and we should be looking at him or her. Then we know that we are not alone, and our tears are seen and heard."[10]

EdRicardo and I made up for the day before by being healing witnesses of each other's pain in this exercise. Amazingly, as much healing as I gained from that profound process, there was still more healing work to be done on the third day of training.

I had no idea how much pain was still inside me about my dad until it came pouring out.

Giving Voice to Everything Unfinished

After having coffee and fruit, and armed with several bags of candy EdRicardo brought to share, we began our final day of training. We continued to explore the topic of "completion" of unresolved issues. How do you complete that which feels incomplete? We learned a critical step in that morning's first exercise. We identified "Recovery Components" and noted them on our timelines.

You'll notice on my relationship review that by each event, the letters A, F, PES, or NES appear. These letters identify "recovery" elements for each memory. In class, we were given three categories: A's for Apologies, F's for Forgiveness, and SES's for Significant Emotional Statements. But in working with clients, I found that breaking the SES's into separate categories of Positive Emotional Statements (PES) and Negative Emotional Statements (NES) made it easier for them to accomplish the final exercise.

These categories are used to identify relationship moments that feel unfinished and the words that need to be spoken for resolution. As *The Grief Recovery Handbook* puts it, they help us "convey any undelivered emotional communication." The tricky part is that most events don't fit neatly into a single category.

Here's an example of an event on my relationship review that fell into all four categories. When I was twenty-five, I went to St. Croix with my parents and my sisters. My mom had a work conference, and the rest of us joined. It was the best vacation ever. We swam with stingrays, lounged on the beach, toured the sugar plantations, and shopped.

Dad wasn't a fan of walking or shopping. Clarification, he was a champion shopper, but not so much if it involved a lot of walking. Our solution was to park him at a bar in town, and then we girls could visit the shops. He'd sit and drink and entertain the locals with his stories. We'd return to drop off packages, and Dad would buy us pina coladas and snacks. One afternoon, he even went to the jewelry store with us and bought us Crucian knot bracelets… an extravagant souvenir from the trip that I cherish to this day. It was so much fun!

After the dinner buffet one night, we went to Walmart, because in the Virgin Islands, that's where you buy rum. And my dad was a big fan of rum. He wanted to bring home the maximum amount allowed by customs because each bottle was less than three dollars! So we loaded up the cart. (Now, as I recall running through the airport, four of us carrying a combined sixteen bottles of rum, I can't help but shake my head and laugh, remembering how much we were willing to do to make Dad happy.)

When checking out at Walmart, the cashier made a mistake and overcharged Dad. The cashier's "solution" was to tell my dad to go to another part of the store to get a credit and return to have the items rung up correctly. He refused.

Dad said, "This was your mistake, and I'm not going to go stand in another line. You need to fix it here." She tried to tell him she couldn't fix it, and she continued to ask him to go elsewhere. He didn't budge.

Meanwhile, the line behind us was growing. My dad didn't notice or care. He kept telling the cashier, "I'm not going anywhere. It was your mistake." The longer this went on, the angrier and louder he became. Everyone was staring at us. I was totally embarrassed! The cashier finally left to find a manager, who thankfully came and fixed the error.

On the way back to the hotel, one of us girls (I can't remember for sure who) made the unfortunate comment, "Well, that was an embarrassing scene." My dad came unglued. He screamed, "*I* wasn't the one who made the mistake! The cashier was the one who messed up!" And so on.

I had so many conflicting feelings surrounding this single event. On one hand, we had such a great time, and I never told my dad or thanked him. On the other hand, he made a huge scene at Walmart and yelled at us in the car. I never expressed my strong positive or negative emotions to my dad. I'd also never forgiven him for his behavior at the store or in the car.

Another thing left unresolved was that I never apologized to my dad for caring about everyone's feelings but his. I was worried about myself, the cashier, and the other people in the store, but not my dad. I could've been more understanding about why he wouldn't change lanes and spend more time walking and standing when he was already worn out from our long day of excursions. I also could have given him credit for saying, "No," when the cashier told him *he* had to be inconvenienced to fix *her* mistake.

So how do we resolve these unfinished emotional experiences? That's where the "Completion Letter" comes in. This letter was our final exercise. I personally prefer to think of it as a Reconciliation Letter because the word "completion" makes people nervous. The moment someone says the words "completion letter," defenses go up: *If you're going to ask me to write a letter to my child and say goodbye, no way! Forget it!* If you're feeling that way now, stay calm.

The letter is *not* goodbye. Rather, it's a means to say all the unsaid things.

In your letter, you express your strong emotions. You apologize and forgive where needed. You address every significant relational event that still leaves you feeling conflicted and carrying pain. But most importantly, as you dwell deeply on the most cherished memories, the turmoil slips away, leaving only peace and love to endure.

Before I began reading my letter to my partner, I closed my eyes and pictured my dad: short black-and-grey hair that in his younger days was wavy and slicked back like Elvis, smiling green eyes, and a white guayabera shirt with its vertical pleats and square hem.

I opened my eyes and there was EdRicardo, brown hair and a white polo shirt, attentive and ready to receive. I took a breath and began to read.

Reconciling With My Dad

Dear Dad,

I've been thinking about our relationship, and I discovered some things I want to say.

Dad, you worked so hard to provide for our family. I never gave you credit or acknowledged your efforts and I apologize for that.

Dad, I have compassion for what you experienced in your childhood. (**)

Dad, when we went to St. Croix, I had so much fun. I really enjoyed being with you and the family. I felt embarrassed when you made a scene at Walmart and hurt when you yelled at us in the car. I forgive you. And I apologize for caring more about what the strangers in Walmart thought than what you felt.

Dad, I felt so angry when you died. You insisted on taking a trip you were not capable of making. If you hadn't done that, you wouldn't have died. I also felt mad about what you put mom through. I forgive you. I didn't really grieve for you very much right after you died. It may have seemed like I didn't care and I apologize.

Dad, when you were in the hospital and I cared for you, it was hard. You were demanding and difficult. And you didn't seem to appreciate my efforts. When you said you would have asked anyone else but me to help you, I felt rejected and unappreciated. I forgive you. We bonded through that experience and for that I'm glad. And I realize now you were thankful in your own way. I apologize for not giving you the benefit of the doubt.

Dad, your angry and temperamental nature caused a lot of tension and stress in our house. I felt scared and afraid of you becoming angry at any moment. I learned to fear conflict, to avoid conflict, and to tolerate bad behavior. This set me up to seek unhealthy relationships. I forgive you.

Dad, your "joking" comments about me having a big butt were hurtful. I was self-conscious about this for 20 years. I forgive you.

Dad, our annual family trips to the beach hold many fond memories for me. When you took me out into the ocean, I felt safe and happy to be with you. Thank you!

Dad, that day after Jackson died, when you sat on the couch with your arm around me and you let me cry, it was very special. Thank you for being there for me and giving me your shoulder to cry on.

Dad, thank you for wanting to be in the delivery room for Jaymeson's birth. You provided comic relief, as always, when you congratulated us on having a bouncing "purple sausage." Thank you for always making us laugh.

Dad, when I walked by your house 2 years after you died and saw your empty lawn chair, I finally really missed you. And that felt good, and right, and peaceful.

I love you. I miss you. Goodbye Dad.

P.S. Dad, being at the hospital with Mom reminded me of something important I didn't say before. In the hospital after you died, that was a very sad but also special moment. We gathered around you. Brenda said she loved your hands, how they always looked the same, no matter your size or age. I remember being confused and asking, "What is that space-age looking thing on his wrist?" A 1st generation Apple watch of course... you always had ALL the gadgets. Before leaving we sang... well, we tried to sing while crying... "Be Not Afraid." You weren't a church-goer Dad. But I believe your spirit was with us and you were glad to hear us sing this song for you. And I'm very thankful to have this memory and to have been there with family as we shared our final moments with you.

I have to go now. I love you. Goodbye, Dad.

———

Reading my letter aloud, I shared with EdRicardo some of the heaviest things I'd carried… things I'd kept to myself for decades.

EdRicardo didn't look away, not down at his lap or out the window, while I choked on my words. He looked directly into my eyes. He saw me. He heard me. In that moment of unfiltered truth, he took my suffering and absorbed it into himself. We sat together feeling the emotional swell of total honesty and vulnerability.

Through his compassion, his brown eyes overflowing with tears for *me*, and his willingness to take the weight of my pain and honor it as if it were his own… *he was my hero.*

Driving home, I reflected on the three-day experience and evaluated how I was feeling. The burden that was lifted and the amount of pain released was indescribable. I felt exhilarated and energized like never before (and I was pretty damn energetic before).

I thought I was doing as well as anyone could after profound loss… healed enough, happy enough.

But now, I felt Glorious.

I sang boisterously with the radio like I was on a Broadway stage, complete with *Glee*-level expressions and hand gestures. I didn't care what other drivers might think or that traffic was stopping up ahead. The sun was drifting down, setting behind Pappadeaux and the giant cowboy boots of North Star Mall.

I sang and rejoiced… in relief for what had been let go and in anticipation of what was to come.

A seismic shift had taken place inside me. Before this weekend in a hotel conference room, I thought I was doing as well as anyone could after profound loss… healed enough, happy enough.

But now, I felt Glorious.

What Makes The Letter Work

Here are a few more details about my letter and why this process works.

Maya Angelou said, *"There is no greater agony than bearing an untold story inside you."*

Writing your letter is a big step, but it's not enough. The words must be spoken, entrusted to a witness who receives them with care. This is when the agony finds relief and pain is transformed into peace.

Reading your letter aloud is essential, but the structure matters too. The paragraphs need to be arranged so that Apologies and Forgiveness come first, along with the corresponding emotional statements. The final portion of the letter is reserved for the purely positive memories (the events on your relationship review that are labeled with PES only). This way, *you close the conversation with an anchor of love, not conflict.*

You may have noticed the statement marked with asterisks (**). I included it to offer compassion to my dad. Some of his difficult traits were due to him growing up very poor, something neither he nor I had any control over. It wasn't something I needed to apologize for or forgive him for, but it felt important to acknowledge his hardship and express empathy.

I'm sure my "goodbye" at the end of the letter didn't slip by you. You might have thought, "Now wait a minute, Jennifer, I thought you said we weren't going to say goodbye." To clarify, this farewell signals the end of this communication only, not the end of the relationship. Think of it like a phone call. When the conversation ends, you say goodbye, yet the connection remains between you.

Finally, the P.S. was added years after I attended training. It's a method for communicating important discoveries that surface later; moments that didn't come to mind during the initial review. The P.S. recognizes that healing doesn't happen in a single moment; it's an ongoing journey. It offers a place to return ensuring nothing important is left unsaid.

———

The stories and reflections I've shared are drawn from my journey through the Grief Recovery Method® program, what I learned, and how it impacted me. If you feel called to experience the program for yourself, I encourage you to connect with the Grief Recovery Institute.

———

New Perspective and Redefining Favorites

Here's one small illustration of how my heart healed and changed. Memories that used to cause pain were now transcended by perspective and peace. As a reminder, I always thought my dad's favorite child was my older sister, Kay. When my little sister was born, 13 years after me, I thought she assumed the title. I never felt like I was his favorite, ever. This journal entry from 2023 shows how my outlook changed.

October 6, 2023

Brenda sent a group text to me and Kay tonight. She had a job interview, and someone asked, "What was your dad like?" She said she panicked because it's hard to describe Dad in a few sentences. She wound up saying, "He was funny! And generous. And... fat." Brenda asked us, "Why did I say that?"

I said, "Because it's true, and our default mode is to tell the truth."

As I thought about the question more, I wondered what dad would have said if he had been asked, "What were your daughters like?"

Kay: "She was my little tank. And my favorite."

Jenni: "She was my little pickles. She talked a lot."

Brenda: "She was my little jellybean. And my favorite."

As I wondered what Dad might have felt about favorites, I remembered one 4th of July when Jayme was a toddler, and we went to a fireworks show. A little girl sat nearby, maybe 4 years old. The fireworks began lighting up the sky, and she exclaimed, "Blue! My favorite!" And then another firework streaked upward and exploded, and she said, "Red! My favorite!" Then another, "Green! My favorite!"

I laughed as she excitedly said every color was her favorite. And I thought, **well, maybe Dad felt that way, too.** Maybe we were all his favorites at different times in different ways.

Then I flashed back to something he said in the hospital when his leg was amputated. We'd been there for several days. And at one point when he was reminiscing about life, he said the weirdest thing. He said, "We were the singers in the family, weren't we Jenni?"

And I was thinking, *What? You sing?* I know he loved music. There was always music playing. He had a radio shaped like a rock by the pool, playing oldies 24/7. And when we sat in the hot tub, he'd turn the speakers up loud. *The Phantom of the Opera* was a big favorite.

But actual singing? I recall one time, when Kay's horse arrived. As the horse walked down the plank, dad sang a rousing chorus, "Hello Dolly, well hello Dolly."

I don't remember him singing anything else. But I'm glad he connected the two of us in his memory that way. I never felt like the favorite. But maybe at least with music and singing (and possibly even other things he didn't tell me), I might have been.

Conclusion

Experiencing the entire process of "grief recovery" was like my own personal exercise in kintsugi.

In re-experiencing and attending to the broken fragments of my past, I smoothed the sharp edges of the shattered pieces. In honoring and sharing the treasured moments, I released pain, repaired brokenness, and filled the cracks with gold.

I was finding my way to being restored… or, another way to look at it — unbroken.

I often wear a pendant like the one pictured below to remind me of how far I've come, how strong I can be, and how Gloriously restored I feel now… with the cracks being, not wounds to be hidden but sacred wonders to be cherished.

Twelve

Guilt and Letting Go

If you could speak to your grief, what would you say? One night in 2022, this question came up for me, and I was struck by how wildly different my answers would be depending upon the day and year.

For the first ten years after Jackson's death, I would've said, "Grief, I'm not dealing with you. I don't have time for you." For many more years I would've said, "Alright, alright you've got my attention. WTF do you want from me?"

Nineteen years later, my journal held an altogether different answer:

> "Thank you, grief. Thank you for continuing to remind me of my beautiful boy, his amazing soul, the time we shared together, and the love that will never leave me. Thank you, grief, for forcing me to address you, learn from you, and be transformed by you. I'm better than I was before you, because of you."

The words surprised me as I wrote them, but they resonated and rang true. I never imagined my answer would be gratitude. Yet here I am… feeling healthy, whole, and even grateful for grief.

If you've been nodding along, you may be wondering how to move toward this kind of healing yourself. One of the biggest hurdles is guilt, clinging and refusing to let go.

The Sticky Hold of Guilt

Virtually all of my grief clients have expressed long-ignored guilt, regret, shame, or some level of responsibility for not saying or doing something different. *I sure did.* We tend to accept these feelings are an unavoidable part of our journey, so guilt hangs on, well after it should have loosened its grip.

Knowledge we acquire today can change what we do tomorrow, but it can't change what we did yesterday.

In 2006, a friend in my SIDS support group was battling a Grief Plunge of guilt. I encouraged her with this impassioned plea:

> We all have things we wish we had done differently, and part of the grief process is to deal with the guilt… and by deal with it I mean accept the fact that we're not perfect and let go of the guilt.
>
> We have to forgive ourselves for whatever actions we initially thought might have been wrong or a mistake and truly know in our hearts that we would **never** have intentionally done anything to harm our babies!
>
> Yes, there are things we know now that we didn't know before, but we can't feel guilty about it. Yes, if we knew then what we know now, we would do things differently, but that's not an option. Knowledge we acquire today can change what we do tomorrow, but it can't change what we did yesterday.

Dang, I really meant all that. But knowing something doesn't necessarily change how you *feel*. I continued to feel guilty for many more years.

Small Details, Big Regrets

To help others haunted by guilt, I wrote this blog post about my guilt… over the tiniest thing:

December 14, 2020

I fed Jackson his early morning feeding at 5:30 a.m., and he went back to sleep. I was returning to a full-time schedule at my job, so I woke him up at 7:30 a.m. to "top him off." He wasn't really all that hungry, so he nursed a bit but then leaned away from my body and looked up at me. I said, "Are you all through?" He gave me a big smile. I said, "You just want to play, don't you?" He smiled again and said, "Oooh." I picked him up and propped him up facing me in the boppy on my knees.

I told him the story of the "Three Little Pigs." He loved that story, especially the part where the big bad wolf said, "Little pigs, little pigs come out!" And the little pigs trembled and said, "Noooooooooohhh, we're not gonna come out."

But, alas, I had to get going or I wasn't going to make it to work until noon! I put him in his blue bouncy seat and threw on some Old Navy jeans, a white sleeveless shirt, a chain belt, and flip flops.

By the time we got to the sitter's house, he was sleepy. I waited on the porch after ringing the bell. I turned the car seat to face me, bounced it on my thigh, and admired his sweet face. He wore a pale-yellow onesie with a beach scene… a red-and-white striped umbrella, a palm tree, and a beach ball. I hadn't put shorts or pants on him. Just white socks.

Debbie answered the door, and I carried the car seat to the couch, setting it on the dark brown velvet cushion. I didn't take him out of his car seat. I could see his eyelids were drooping, and he might fall asleep if I didn't disturb him. Oh, how I wish I had taken him out, held him one last time.

Ever since that day, I've wondered if things would've been different if I had gotten him out of the car seat to play for a while rather than go down for a nap and never wake up again. Would he have lived if I hadn't put socks on him? It was early June… probably too hot for socks. Overheating, I learned after the fact, is a factor in Sudden Infant Death Syndrome.

Why on earth did I put socks on him? Another one of the endless Why's and What If's. In reading about child loss, I learned that all parents feel guilty about their child's death. The guilt is inevitable because we think we should've sensed something was wrong and done something differently. Our job was to take care of our child, and we didn't do it. Thus, no matter the circumstances, we feel guilty.

I also learned that in MOST cases, the parent, of course, had no way of knowing anything was amiss, nor the ability to change their behavior in any way that would alter the outcome. In the FEW cases when the parent may have done something that *could* have been a factor, in almost every one of those cases, the parent was *not aware* of doing harm nor doing anything *intentionally* to cause harm. They may have been uninformed on a certain topic (as I was about SIDS), but they didn't do anything on purpose to cause harm. Therefore, the guilt is unfounded.

A quote widely attributed to Maya Angelou sums this up, saying, "Forgive yourself for not knowing what you didn't know before you learned it." But we can't get to the balmy relief of that truth until we confront our guilt.

Even though I intellectually know I didn't cause Jackson's death or do anything wrong *per se*, I regret the socks to this day. What I feel now isn't guilt, but it's not 100% acceptance either.

Here's the mantra I've chosen (again and again because guilt is like heartburn… always flaring up no matter what you do to avoid it): *"I did the best I could with the information and resources I had at the time."*

If you feel guilty for not predicting or preventing your loved one's death, I hope you'll embrace my mantra, too. Odds are, there's nothing you could have done differently to change what happened.

You did the best you could with the resources you had… and a crystal ball wasn't one of them.

Happy 21st Birthday to My 89-Day-Old Son

Letting go of my guilt opened the door to savoring my most cherished memories of Jackson. The saddest ones are still sad, and they always will be, but remembering doesn't plunge me back to Gutted. There's beauty in bringing him with me in my life and in my heart, which has been restored piece by piece, so I can live and love Gloriously.

Here's what I wrote and shared with my email subscribers in honor of his 21st birthday, on March 7, 2024.

"Rocking" by Olivia Newton John was one of my favorite songs to sing to my newborn baby Jackson, "Precious baby, sweetly sleep, do not cry, I will sing a lullaby. I will rock you, rock you, rock you." These lyrics transport me into an alternate universe. A universe of unimagined joy and pain.

I rocked him and sang to him every night. Until he disappeared. He was just gone. I stood in the hallway at the hospital, holding a chocolate-brown stuffed puppy with "his dates" written on the tag, and the ground fell out from underneath my feet.

The earth opened, and what used to be the ground fell away, and I plummeted into the hole… and kept falling. The essence of me fell away too, just like the ground that abandoned me and left me nowhere to put my feet.

We played the "Rocking" song at his funeral. Before the service began, my friend Jan came striding down the aisle. She was wearing the brightest multicolored shirt and skirt I've ever seen… hot pink and bright orange and turquoise blue. Like a Hawaiian beach towel in technicolor. Some may have thought it was a bad choice, but I loved that she didn't wear black, beige, or some other lifeless color.

As she was hugging me, she said, "I'm so sorry Jennifer. I can't imagine. Please let me know if there's anything I can do." Then the song came on. The service was about to start.

Tears began to flow. Mine and so many more. I saw neighbors from down the street, friends I'd worked with for years, my sisters, and my mom… sobbing and trying to breathe. *We were never going to see him or hold him again.*

During those days of non-stop activity, planning the funeral and the visitation, choosing scriptures and songs, a casket, his burial plot, somehow I thought if I could just get through all this, life would go back to normal.

I didn't think beyond the burial. I guess that's the shock and denial of grief. When the services were over and everyone went back to their regular lives, I began the journey to figure out how to live without my son.

He's buried under a huge oak tree that drapes protectively over the sacred ground.

There's a black and gray speckled granite bench where I sit and talk to him and sing our favorite songs.

On the side of the bench these words are inscribed:

Precious baby, sweetly sleep. Until I see you again, my darling, I'll continue to cherish and celebrate your birth and the 89 halcyon days you were here in my arms.

———

I've celebrated Jackson's birthday in some fashion for 21 years. I hope knowing this gives you the inspiration, permission, and confidence you need to continue your relationship with your loved one. To keep talking and sharing when your heart is overflowing. Keep remembering. Keep honoring the special days.

Celebrate your loved one boldly, reminding the world that their life mattered and always will.

CONCLUSION

HANGING ON: A STORY OF SURVIVAL, SOMEDAY, AND SEARCHING FOR PEACE

A Tiny Hero

One night before bed, while writing this book, I reflected on life, as I tend to do. I thought about life lessons, getting older… big things I would prefer to think about at other times but, this is what I do. Anyway, I was thinking about how difficult it was to answer people who would learn about Jackson and then ask, "*How* did you survive the death of your child?"

An episode of *60 Minutes* from ages ago, before I was married or had kids, popped into my head. The program featured a five or six-year-old girl, who didn't want her dad to leave her at home while he drove into town. So, as he went out the front door, she sneaked out behind him. He walked to their van and got inside. But she didn't open the passenger door… instead she climbed onto the bumper.

Her dad proceeded down the road, five miles into town. When he arrived, he found his daughter sitting on the bumper, to which she clung.

The *60 Minutes* interviewer asked the girl, *"How* did you hold on so long as your dad drove five miles?"

"TIGHT!" she said, her mouth stretched wide, baring tiny teeth. She raised her clenched fists and squinched up her eyes to convey the extreme effort. I laughed so hard at her simple yet descriptive reply.

Parallels

Unlike the little girl's simple answer, my answer to *"How* did you survive?"* was a complex evolution. For years, I felt like people were asking me the question while I was still hanging on to a moving vehicle for dear life.

Early on, I'm not sure how I answered. Maybe I wasn't sure surviving was guaranteed, though that's what I was trying to do.

But it would have been accurate to say, "DETERMINATION!" or "NO CHOICE IN THE MATTER!" while scrunching up my face and fisting my hands just like the little girl.

Clinging to Someday

With hindsight, a more descriptive answer is reflected in a poem I wrote:

HOW?
I forced myself to believe in someday.
Someday I would feel better.
Someday I would be happy again.
Someday I would care about ordinary things like watching
TV and eating.
Someday I would look forward to what the future might hold.
Someday I wouldn't feel so afraid.
Someday I would heal.
Someday I would find peace.

Someday was my consolation and my motivation. Boy, did I have *a lot* riding on someday. And, not to sound boastful, but I was right.

Someday did come, bringing those small yet wondrous everyday joys, watershed moments of growth and healing, and…

… peace.

Grasping for Peace

Now peace can be tricky. A few years ago, even with all the work and healing I'd done, I hadn't made it all the way to whole-hearted peace.

My coach asked me one day to journal the answer to this question: "Is peace a component of your life after loss?"

Here's what I wrote:

May 23, 2021

Oh, boy, this gives me great pause. Peace is a hard word to agree with. It's a hard thing to think is possible. I know a certain level of peace now that I've been through grief recovery. Before that, I think I would have said "No way. It's just not possible. I've come a long way, but I can't get to peace. Because that sounds like total acceptance, 100% okay with my son being dead, and I'm not."

I mean, I live with the fact that he's dead. And I've made a concerted effort to live with the reality of that gracefully, faithfully, and eventually, even being able to be truly happy again. But I've never felt that I was completely fine with Jackson being absent from the world.

I'm not "over it" and I don't think I ever will be. Maybe peace doesn't mean being over it or okay with it. But then what does peace mean? I have peace with God. I'm not angry at him or wondering why he did this to me anymore.

Sometimes, I think peace means what it says in that song, "It is well, with my soul." But I can't say that. I can't say, regarding my son dying, that it is well with my soul.

I can say my soul is well. And that is phenomenal progress.

But my soul is still not well if we are specifically talking about my son's death. That's a different thing. Or maybe it's not. Just right now, to me, it feels like a different thing.

Finally Getting a Grip

Reflecting on my progress in the last few years, I'm surprised. Because today, the word "peace" doesn't feel so sharp or offensive. It feels softer. And I feel softer, having a sense of peace I didn't have before. I don't know if I'm 100% there yet. But I'm moving in that direction.

I want you to know that someday, your soul *can* find peace and rest. I realize "someday" is a vague timeline and probably not as comforting as you might like, but it's for sure. "Someday" has big, beautiful things in store for you.

Just like that determined little girl clinging to the bumper, sometimes all we can do is hold on *tight*. And like each of those five miles must have felt interminable to her, the journey through grief can feel endless. Remember, every Grief Plunge and Grief Float through the 6 G's brings you closer to healing, restoration, and the Glorious life ahead.

On those days when you think you can't take another step, try clenching your fists and holding on to hope with all your might. "Someday" will arrive and bring the peace you long for.

"When you are sorrowful, look again in your heart and you shall see that in truth you are weeping for that which has been your delight."

— Kahlil Gibran

EPILOGUE

At a writing retreat, days before turning in this manuscript, I announced to my author friends, "The book is done. I feel complete."

Yet, on the drive home, one more story niggled in the back of my brain. The story kept coming to mind, through the night and the next day.

I countered the pesky thought, "No, I'm at the maximum word count. I'd have to re-work everything to create space for this story. I'm tired. I need to be done."

My inner voice insisted, "This story is important and you need to add it into the book."

Thus, I wrote this Epilogue… to share with you a profound truth that hit me in 2023.

I wrote about it first in my journal and later shared it with my community. Here's how it unfolded.

June 4, 2023 — Journal Entry

I listened to Rick Warren on Carey Nieuwhof's podcast yesterday.

He was sharing about his son who battled depression for many years and ultimately gave up the fight when he died by suicide.

Rick said what gave him the most comfort was

receiving cards from hundreds of people who said his son had led them to Jesus before his passing.

One morning, Rick sat in the garden writing in his journal, and these words came to him:

"In God's garden of grace, even broken trees bear fruit. And we're all broken."

That hit me powerfully. Even broken trees bear fruit. And we're all broken.

I thought I was broken forever. But God had a purpose and a plan to help me redeem the pain and put my broken pieces back together.

Now, I'm twenty years into this journey, finally able to bear fruit. I can share my story and give hope to those who are stuck, scared, or feeling desperately alone.

That journal entry kept tugging at me. A few days later, I drafted this message to my readers:

Excerpt from email (June 7, 2023)
No matter where you are on your journey, no matter how broken you may feel, you too will find purpose and bear fruit.

Maybe you're in a season where you need to tend to your own brokenness. Maybe you're showing up for your family or your job and giving it everything you've got.

Or maybe, you're farther along and starting to wonder if there's something more you're meant to do.

Wherever you are, it's exactly where you need to be.

In God's garden of grace, broken things aren't barren... they have value, beauty, and purpose.

When you feel doubtful or defeated, remember:

You've come a long way. You're doing great. And you're not done yet.

With all my broken-yet-beautiful love,
Jennifer

RESOURCES

You made it. You reached the end of this book. I'm so honored to have had your time and (hopefully rapt) attention as I shared the details of my personal losses, lessons, and transformation.

I'm proud of you. It takes courage to face the hardest parts of your life and your big emotions in search of hope and healing. More than anything, my fervent wish is that you feel motivated to live "gloriously alive" instead of "alive enough."

Before you close this book, let's make sure you know your next step.

As my friend Jodi Wellman says (in *You Only Die Once*), "... a dream without a plan is just a wish accompanied by a lot of sauvignon blanc." For me, it would be red zinfandel, but either way, she's right. You need a plan.

You've come this far. Don't leave your grief transformation to chance. Keep going!

After everything we've been through together in these pages, I hope it's safe to say we're not strangers... perhaps even friends.

So from one soul who's known deep grief to another, I invite you to decide on the next step. Just pick one thing to make sure you keep moving forward.

Quick Wins

1. Read my ebook *How to Shut Down the Unrelenting Question, "WHY, God?"*
2. Download Excel templates to guide your own Loss Review/ Relationship Review.
3. Read a booklet of entries from my personal *Letters to Jackson* journal.

Stay Connected

1. Sign up for my email newsletter for stories, insights, and inspiration.
2. Follow me on Substack for fresh reflections, real-time stories, and exclusive content I don't share anywhere else.
3. Receive 1-3 grief support texts each week providing hope, resources, and encouragement.

Go Deeper

1. Download journal prompts to Tell Your Grief Story Through the 6 G's: Prompts designed to help you reflect, process, heal, and maybe even begin sharing your story in a newsletter, Substack, or book.
2. Join the 6-month Grief Companion journey: Weekly emails and personalized responses with compassionate support, tools, and practical advice.
3. Get on the waitlist for my Transform Your Life After Loss® Retreat: A two-day experience designed to help you release a lifetime of unresolved pain so you can stop just existing and start pursuing your goals and dreams again.

Links to all resources can be found at jenniferhacker.com/ everything

Remember, you don't have to do it all… just choose one thing. As the Chinese proverb says, "A journey of a thousand miles begins with a single step."

I'm here cheering you on, for the first step, and every step that follows.

Scan for Resources

———

Give Back

If your heart is stirred to help others and you have the financial ability, please consider donating to my non-profit organization:

The Center for Help and Hope

https://thecenterforhelpandhope.org

Our mission is to improve the mental and emotional health of women experiencing major life transitions by providing educational resources, financial assistance, and affordable coaching services.

Our vision is a world where women are fully resourced and supported through life transitions thereby improving not only their own health but the health and stability of their families. Increasing the number of healthy families is key to positive change in society.

Acknowledgments

To the amazing team at Ignite Press: Everett O'Keefe, Malia Sexton, and Zelda Fogle. Thank you for your guidance, skill, and belief in the message of this book. A special thank you to Everett for championing its value from the very beginning and for sharing your insights so generously, especially through your book *The Power of the Published*. It confirmed that pouring my words onto the page was worth the effort… because those words carry purpose, power, and lasting impact.

To my Advance Praise Readers: Jodi Wellman, Mary Pritzlaff, Rebecca Thorne, Jane Carter, Samantha Kriegel, Sandra Frost, and Samantha Anna. Thank you for your thoughtful feedback and life-giving encouragement.

To my A-List Author sisters, Sandy Evenson and MaryAnn Gramig: Your insight and enthusiasm kept me going.

To my brilliant book coach, Cindy Childress, PhD: Thank you for turning chaos into clarity. Without your guidance, this book would still be scattered across spiral notebooks, Evernote files, emails, post-its, and scraps of paper. Thank you for your unwavering belief in me and my story and for helping me hone my author skills.

To Diana Long, my instructor at the Life Purpose Institute and coach: You taught me how to guide others with skill and heart. You helped me envision, and create, a new and beautiful chapter of life.

To Susan Dindinger: Thank you for your kind and skilled

instruction in the Grief Recovery Method®. Your compassionate presence and guidance opened the door to a kind of healing I didn't know was possible. I'm forever grateful.

To my Helotes CrossFit family, especially owners Rick and Angela Damiano; the fantastic coaches; and my HCF sisters: Kristen Logan (the OG), Beverly Bloom, Elsa Coates, April Garcia, and Laura Wallington. And to *every* member, you matter to me. I could not have survived without this community. I mean that quite literally.

To my Soul Sisters, in chronological order because I could never rank the impact you've had: Sheila Strickland Wray, Schawn Keener Wreden, Samantha Anna, Stacy Shuman Sparks, and Samantha Kriegel. My life has been profoundly impacted by each of you, more than you know. I love you deeply and forever.

To EdRicardo Gandara, my grief recovery partner: You showed up as a champion for a stranger. You stepped in with courage and kindness and gave me a gift that changed everything. You'll always be my hero.

To my niece Abby Mueller: You were my eyes when I could no longer see straight. Your careful attention to detail was a life-saving gift that helped bring this book across the finish line.

To my brother Mitch and sister-in-law Lorinda: You stood with me through every moment of the worst week of my life. Mitch, I'll always remember the love and courage it took to write and deliver the eulogy, and I'm grateful for the gift of your willingness to carry that burden for me and our family. Lorinda, thank you for your steady support, for always asking about the book, responding to every call to action, and boldly reminding me how proud you are. Your encouragement has been a bright light.

To my sister Brenda: You showed up on my doorstep when I didn't even know how much I needed you. You had wisdom beyond your years and brought laughter into the fog of grief. You had the courage to have hard conversations most people avoid. And you never stopped remembering Jackson, sending notes and texts, years and years after his death.

To my sister Kay: You showed me how to listen, how to be a true friend, and what it looks like to be an extraordinary mother. You took care of me so beautifully after Jackson was born (and many times thereafter). Your nurturing presence is always a comfort.

Dad, you still make us laugh, even from beyond the grave. When we're together, your one-of-a-kind personality and legendary stories come rushing back… vivid, hilarious, and a reminder that you're never really gone.

Mom, thank you for the countless sacrifices you made to raise what you call "the best family in the whole world." I know you don't say that to brag, but because you feel blessed. The truth is, so much of what makes our family special traces back to your example, the values you instilled in us, and your unconditional love and acceptance.

To Jaymeson and Jake: Thank you for your patience, your support, and for putting up with all the times I said, "I'm almost done" and I absolutely wasn't. Your sacrifice and encouragement mean the world to me. I'm endlessly proud and grateful to be your mom. I love you to the moon and back.

To Johnny: You've been the sun, air, and rain… essential elements that made it possible for me to grow and bloom. I could never have done this without your love, belief, and steady strength. I love you more than I can express.

———

And for anyone I've unintentionally left off this list, I created a dedicated space where I'll make updates to honor and thank everyone who contributed to this book and my journey. Visit **jenniferhacker.com/thanks**.

Review Inquiry

Hey, it's Jennifer.

If this book helped you, would you give it a quick rating or review where you bought it?

Online bookstores promote books with strong reader feedback, and your review really helps others find this message.

1. Go to the retailer where you purchased your copy.
2. Search my name and the book title.
3. Leave a rating or short review.
4. (Optional) Add a photo of you with the book - readers love seeing those.

Thank you so much,

Jennifer

WILL YOU SHARE THE LOVE?

If this book was valuable to you, consider gifting a copy to someone who needs it.

Bulk pricing is available for teams, groups, and organizations. Just send an email to **info@jenniferhacker.com**.

Endnotes

1. https://aspe.hhs.gov/sites/default/files/documents/1ed9790d93a64e9054e0b25b808f0eff/bereavement-grief-services-report-congress-2023.pdf
2. https://pmc.ncbi.nlm.nih.gov/articles/PMC10320710/
3. https://www.psychiatry.org/patients-families/prolonged-grief-disorder
4. https://www.centerforloss.com/2022/04/grief-is-not-a-disorder/
5. https://www.cbsnews.com/news/brene-brown-cope-coronavirus-pandemic-covid-19-60-minutes-2020-03-29/?ftag=CNM-00-10aab5j&linkId=85359119&fbclid=IwAR3OgZEbRRifDeC9mm7P6E0uZdmbZe_vcErHeZPvUtisJWyOnfijEfzDwLI
6. https://whatsyourgrief.com/embracing-the-strength-of-weak-ties/
7. https://www.instagram.com/p/C-fx4nkOdlP/?utm_source=ig_web_copy_link&igsh=MzRlODBiNWFlZA==
8. https://brenebrown.com/transcript/david-kessler-and-brene-on-grief-and-finding-meaning/
9. https://www.psychologytoday.com/us/blog/from-surviving-to-thriving/201904/posttraumatic-growth
10. https://www.cloudtownsend.com/suffering-and-grief/

REFERENCE LIST

A Grief Observed by C.S. Lewis

A Heart That Works by Rob Delaney

Atomic Habits by James Clear

Carey Nieuwhof Leadership Podcast (episodes 409 and 467 with Rick Warren)

Find Your People: Building Deep Community in a Lonely World by Jennie Allen

Finding Meaning: The Sixth Stage of Grief by David Kessler

Healing After Loss: Daily Meditations for Working Through Grief by Martha Hickman

Healing a Parent's Grieving Heart by Alan Wolfelt

I Know Why the Caged Bird Sings by Maya Angelou

It's OK That You're Not OK: Meeting Grief and Loss in a Culture That Doesn't Understand by Megan Devine

Joy Is My Justice: Reclaim What Is Yours by Tanmeet Sethi

Knowing: Memoirs of a journey beyond the veil and choosing joy after tragic loss by Jeffery Olsen

On Death and Dying by Elisabeth Kübler-Ross

Permission to Mourn: A New Way to do Grief by Tom Zuba

Soundtracks: The Surprising Solution to Overthinking by Jon Acuff

The Body Keeps the Score: Brain, Mind, and Body in the Healing of Trauma by Bessel van der Kolk

The Bregdan Chronicles by Ginny Dye

The Grief Recovery Handbook by John James and Russell Friedman

The Prophet by Kahlil Gibran

The Two Towers by J.R.R. Tolkien

Unattended Sorrow by Stephen Levine

What's Your Grief? (website, podcast, and blog by Eleanor Haley and Litsa Williams)

When Bad Things Happen to Good People by Harold Kushner

You Only Die Once: How to Make It to the End with No Regrets by Jodi Wellman

Nationwide 988 Suicide & Crisis Lifeline: (1-800-273-TALK (8255)

About the Author

J ennifer Hacker is an author, Grief Coach, and founder of the 6 G's of Grief Transformation. She specializes in helping clients heal unresolved pain and move into their purpose and joy *without* moving on. Her clients appreciate her deep empathy, her insight and unique perspectives on grief, her encouragement and ability to kindle  hope in the darkest moments, and her attentive and active listening, which makes them feel safe to unpack even the most painful losses.

Her passion is educating people about the mistaken beliefs about grief that are pervasive in our culture which cause grievers to become stuck, living with deep unhealed wounds. She has experienced this first-hand, having lost her infant son to SIDS, and then navigating a nineteen-year journey from Gutted to Glorious. Jennifer shares her story to inspire others to believe they, too, can be restored and live a glorious life after loss.

Before her coaching career, she spent 20+ years working as an Accountant, CFO, and CEO. Then, her numerous personal losses and unresolved pain ultimately led to her next chapter. While she loved her business career, she felt a calling to do *more* to help women in need. She quit her corporate job and became an ICF Certified Life Coach and GRI Certified Grief Specialist.

Jennifer founded the Center for Help and Hope, a non-profit organization that supports women navigating pivotal life transitions and loss. She lives in San Antonio, TX with her partner Johnny, her son Jake, and her fluffy companion Orion. Her daughter Jayme is a senior at Texas A&M University. She loves CrossFit, reading, singing, and family trips to the beach.

Jennifer can be reached at: **jennifer@jenniferhacker.com**